At Issue

Negative Campaigning

Other Books in the At Issue Series:

At Issue

| Negative Campaigning

Margaret Haerens, Book Editor

GREENHAVEN PRESS
A part of Gale, Cengage Learning

Farmington Hills, Mich • San Francisco • New York • Waterville, Maine
Meriden, Conn • Mason, Ohio • Chicago

Elizabeth Des Chenes, *Director, Content Strategy*
Cynthia Sanner, *Publisher*
Douglas Dentino, *Manager, New Product*

For more information, contact:
Greenhaven Press
27500 Drake Rd.
Farmington Hills, MI 48331-3535
Or you can visit our Internet site at gale.cengage.com

ISBN 978-0-7377-6846-6 (hardcover)
ISBN 978-0-7377-6847-3 (pbk.)

Library of Congress Cataloging in Publication Control Number: 2013044341

Printed in the United States of America
1 2 3 4 5 6 7 18 17 16 15 14

Contents

Introduction

In the last few months of 2011, a scathing thirty-minute film attacking the business record of 2012 presidential candidate Mitt Romney began making the rounds of Republican political circles. Titled *When Mitt Romney Came to Town*, the polemical video was created by a former Romney advisor and condemned Romney's tenure as CEO of Bain Capital, a private investment firm, as a ruthless assault on American economic security. It focuses on the negative consequences for four US companies after being bought out by Bain under Romney's tenure: UniMac, which produced commercial laundry equipment; KB Toys, a chain of retail toy stores; DDI, an electronics company; and AmPad, an office supply producer.

When Mitt Romney Came to Town paints Romney as a greedy corporate raider intent on killing the American dream. "Capitalism made America great," the narrator begins.

> "Free markets. Innovation. Hard work. The building blocks of the American dream. But in the wrong hands, some of those dreams can turn into nightmares. Wall Street's corporate raiders made billions of dollars. . . . Their greed was matched only by their willingness to do anything to make millions in profits. Nothing spared. Nothing mattered but greed. This film is about one such raider and his firm. . . . For tens of thousands of Americans, the suffering began when Mitt Romney came to town." [1]

When Mitt Romney Came to Town posed a potential threat to the Romney campaign, which was in the midst of a bruising primary battle with several Republican opponents to become the party's 2012 presidential candidate. It struck at Romney's business experience and portrayed him as a cold-blooded Wall Street financier—one of the men responsible for sending American jobs overseas while making large profits for themselves and their companies. In a country still feeling the

1. http://www.youtube.com/watch?v=BLWnB9FGmWE.

effects of the 2007–2009 economic downturn, the campaign officials recognized that the video could resonate with American voters and turn them against Romney.

In January 2012, the rights to *When Mitt Romney Came to Town* were purchased by Winning Our Future, a Super PAC that supported Newt Gingrich, one of Romney's rivals for the Republican presidential nomination. Winning Our Future outbid a number of other Super PACs for the right to release the video to media outlets. The video's release during the primary campaign did not change the outcome of the primary process—Romney still won the Republican presidential nomination—but it garnered much publicity over Bain's controversial business record and Romney's role in sending American jobs overseas. It reinforced an image of Romney as a rich, out-of-touch Wall Street raider with little concern for the average American—an image later exploited by his Democratic opponent, Barack Obama.

Political scientists are still evaluating the impact Super PACs like Winning Our Future had on the 2012 presidential election. What is clear is that this relatively new kind of political advocacy organization was changing political campaigns and influencing the US electoral process in ways unseen in previous elections. According to filings by the Federal Election Commission (FEC), a total of 266 Super PACs spent more than $546 million dollars on political ads during the 2012 election. Much of this spending was focused on negative ads against specific presidential, Senate, or congressional candidates—a trend that was bound to have a significant effect on national, state, and even local elections.

Super PACS are a new phenomenon, created by two controversial 2010 court decisions: *Citizens United v. Federal Election Commission* and *Speechnow.org v. Federal Election Commission*. Before these two decisions were handed down, there were only political action committees (PACs), not Super PACs, which were heavily regulated groups that could raise money to support a specific candidate or cause from individuals, not corporations or unions. According to campaign financing laws, each individual could only donate a total of $2,500 to a specific PAC.

On January 21, 2010, the Supreme Court decision in *Citizens United* changed those rules. The Court struck down all caps on individual donations and decided that corporations and unions could also make unlimited contributions. In his majority opinion, Justice Anthony Kennedy asserted that "Speech is an essential mechanism of democracy, for it is the means to hold officials accountable to the people. . . . The right of citizens to inquire, to hear, to speak, and to use information to reach consensus is a precondition to enlightened self-government and a means to protect it."[2]

A few months later, the United States Court of Appeals for the District of Columbia Circuit issued a decision in *Speechnow.org v. Federal Election Commission* allowing for the creation of "independent expenditure-only" groups, which became known as Super PACs. These groups may raise unlimited contributions from corporations, unions, associations, and individuals, then spend unlimited funds to advocate for or against political candidates. However, Super PACs are prohibited from directly donating to the campaigns of political candidates.

These 2010 court rulings subsequently led to a proliferation of Super PACs. As of August 2013, there were 1,310 such groups registered with the FEC. These Super PACs have been created and funded to advocate for a range of candidates and issues, including strengthening America's ties with China and Israel; supporting the political interests of various industries; and seeking to elect or defeat President Barack Obama. There are Super PACs for education, the environment, immigration, and the flat tax. There are several for state horse associations and even a Super PAC established by the comedian Stephen

2. http://www.supremecourt.gov/opinions/09pdf/08-205.pdf.

Colbert, whose Americans for a Better Tomorrow, Tomorrow raised around $1.25 million until it was dissolved in 2012.

One of the initial impacts of Super PACs on the 2012 election was the trend of wealthy donors contributing millions of dollars to fund negative campaign ads, sometimes blanketing swing states with ads in support of specific candidates. This has raised concerns that millionaires and billionaires are buying more and more control over the political process. Another is the ability of Super PACs to finance the production and distribution of short online films, such as *When Mitt Romney Came to Town*, that closely examine and amplify criticisms about certain candidates. Some commentators regard Super PACs as the "attack dogs" of the 2012 election campaign, doing the dirty work that the candidates and their campaign organizations did not want to do.

At Issue: Negative Campaigning examines the roles of Super PACs and the *Citizens United* decision on American electoral politics. Other viewpoints included in the volume debate the efficacy and history of negative campaigning, the influence of fact-checking on political campaigning, and the impact of negative campaigning on the 2012 US presidential election.

1

Negative Campaigning Is Effective

Drew Westen

Drew Westen is a professor of psychology and psychiatry at Emory University and the author of The Political Brain: The Role of Emotion in Deciding the Fate of the Nation (2007).

Political candidates rely on negative campaigning because it works. Although people say that they don't like negative ads, studies have shown that they trigger negative associations about certain candidates that persist and intensify over time. It is imperative that political candidates activate both negative and positive emotions and craft a campaign that attracts voters to them, while steering voters away from political opponents. Negative campaigning does not have to be extreme; it can contain just a kernel of truth for it to resonate with voters. Candidates who understand how emotions work and how the brain processes negative messages and imagery will have an advantage over their opponents.

In poll after poll, Americans say they don't like negative campaigning. Yet in the final week of the Florida primary, more than 90% of the ads broadcast were attack ads. That's not likely to change in the run-up to Super Tuesday [March 6, 2012].

So why do candidates rely so heavily on a kind of advertising voters say they abhor?

Because it works. To understand why, you have to consider what we know about how emotions work—and the different ways our conscious and unconscious minds and brains process "negativity" during elections.

Researching Attack Ads

In 2008, my colleague Joel Weinberger and I tested voters' conscious and unconscious responses to two ads. The first was an anti-Barack Obama ad of Hillary Rodham Clinton's. "It's 3 a.m., and your children are safe and asleep," it began, "but there's a phone in the White House and it's ringing." It then went on to suggest that Clinton, because of her seasoning in national politics, was far better qualified to answer that phone than the less-experienced Obama.

The second was an anti-John McCain ad put out by the Campaign to Defend America. It was designed to suggest that a vote for McCain was a vote for four more years of George W. Bush policies. The ad juxtaposed the policies promoted by the two men and interchanged their heads, concluding that the Republican nominee was "McSame as Bush."

There's nothing like a sinister portrayal of a greedy, self-centered villain, replete with grainy images and menacing music, to stir up our unconscious minds.

The voters we surveyed claimed to despise both ads, describing them in focus groups as "pandering." They insisted the ads would backfire with them. But using a well-established method for assessing which words the commercials activated unconsciously, we discovered that although voters consciously disliked both commercials, the ads were nevertheless highly effective. Both "stuck," triggering negative associations with Obama and McCain in the minds of most viewers, including those who thought they were unaffected. When viewing the face of Obama, the words most strongly activated by the "3 a.m." ad were "weak," "lightweight," "terrorist" and "Muslim." The word that stuck unconsciously after the "McSame" ad was "Bush."

Viewers may have rejected the ads consciously, but that doesn't mean they weren't unconsciously affected.

The Challenge of Negative Campaign Ads

Our conscious reactions reflect our conscious values. In the case of campaigns, for most people, those values include a belief that people should run on their merits and stop tearing each other down. But unconsciously, our brains are highly reactive to threat—especially when, as in the case of an ad, the threat isn't immediately countered or refuted. A well-crafted positive ad can "stick" too, but there's nothing like a sinister portrayal of a greedy, self-centered villain, replete with grainy images and menacing music, to stir up our unconscious minds.

Attack ads have pros and cons in a primary. On one hand, they can do great damage to a candidate who may ultimately be the party's choice. [Mitt] Romney is the target of both Newt Gingrich and Rick Santorum now, but if the former Massachusetts governor ultimately gets the Republican nomination, the party will want voters to forget all the primary attacks. And his own attack ads in Florida against Gingrich—which were highly effective—created negative associations to him too. The plus side to these kinds of early attacks is that they come far enough in advance of the election that they may feel like old news come November. Moreover, they give candidates a preview of attacks that will likely come from the other party in the general election and allow them to prepare responses in advance. Gingrich's attacks in Florida, for example, forced Romney to find a better answer to charges that he is a "vulture capitalist" who earned his money by putting people out of work.

It's ironic that so much attention is now being focused on the impact of Gingrich's attack ads, which seem to have left the unlikely Santorum as the latest beneficiary of Republican anti-Romney sentiments. In Iowa, Gingrich was leading in the polls until his rivals began hitting him with one attack after another. He chose not to respond, taking voters at their word that they wanted a positive campaign. That was a rookie error, particularly striking for a veteran politician who had made his way to the top of the GOP leader board with his razor-sharp debate responses, and who had spent a career as a professional gadfly, never shy to take a shot at anyone, even Ronald Reagan.

Gingrich's refusal to answer the attacks may have reflected the hubris that has so often been his undoing, or it may have stemmed from an admonition by his pollsters that a tit-for-tat campaign would drive up his already sky-high negatives with swing voters. But whatever the reasoning, it was wrongheaded if he wanted to win—and the once front-runner found himself a distant third in the Iowa caucuses.

Using Emotion in Political Campaigns

Every political strategist knows that there are four stories you have to control if you want to win an election: the story you're telling about yourself, the story your opponent is telling about himself, the story your opponent is telling about you, and the story you're telling about your opponent. Gingrich lost Iowa because he was talking only about himself—ignoring the unflattering picture the other candidates were painting of him and failing to speak to the legitimate weaknesses of his rivals.

The reason it's so crucial for politicians to activate both negative and positive emotions is that they are not, as our intuition would suggest, just opposites. Emotions such as anxiety, fear and disgust involve very different neural circuits than, say, happiness or enthusiasm. A candidate's job is to get all those neural circuits firing, both the ones that draw voters in and the ones that push them away from other candidates.

That doesn't require making things up about your adversaries. You don't have to bend the truth too far to paint a worrisome picture of any of the candidates this year—or to present an image that's positive (at least with some creative air-brushing).

But in hard times with flawed candidates, expect a lot of negative campaign ads between now and November.

2

Despite the Bluster, Negative Campaign Ads Ineffective

Peter Callaghan

Peter Callaghan is a political reporter for The News Tribune *in Tacoma, Washington.*

There is a prevalent belief that negative campaigning is effective. However, studies show that its impact is mixed. The assumption that negative campaigns work is driven by political campaigns that spend large amounts of money on attack ads and by political consultants justifying large salaries. In reality, negative campaigning is likely to drive down voter turnout. Another problem is that the definition of a negative campaign ad is murky: for some voters, a particular ad is dirty and vicious because it insults their candidate; for others, the same ad is perceived as necessary to draw contrast between two candidates and their positions on specific issues.

What's the difference between a negative campaign ad and a "contrast" ad? It's negative if it attacks your side and a contrast ad if it's aimed at the other guys.

Oversimplified? Maybe a little. But too many voters define negative ads as the dirty, vicious attacks on their candidate, the kind of campaigning that should be condemned, even banned. Contrast ads are seen as a necessary act of holding the other candidate accountable for who they are, what they say, what they believe and who they may have been associated with no matter how peripherally.

An Assault of Attack Ads

We'll get more fodder than we might want—some on TV but also in the mailbox, over the phone, by email or via social media. And while we might feel assaulted, just think of our fellow citizens in the shrinking number of presidential battleground states. *The Washington Post* reported recently that 115,000 ads had already run in Ohio compared with 43,000 over the same period in 2008. Super PACs get most of the blame, but neither candidate is accepting federal funding and its cap on spending while Republican John McCain accepted the money four years ago.

Here in the presidential backwaters, I guess we can put up with that woman talking about Rob McKenna [the unsuccessful Republican candidate for attorney general of Washington in 2012] as though he's someone she met in a bar. ("You know how you meet someone? He seems nice enough. You think, 'Well, maybe.' Then you actually check him out online, and he isn't at all who he says he is. Republican Rob McKenna is one of those guys.") And because it can't possibly go on forever, I can tolerate hearing five old white guys—clearly the demographic that'll put the Republicans over the top—complain about Jay Inslee [currently the governor of Washington] before telling the kids to get off their lawn.

The assumption behind negative campaigning is that it must work. Research is mixed, though.

I sat on a panel recently sponsored by Humanities Washington called "Dirty Business: A History of Negative Campaigning." A college professor, TVW [a public service network] president Greg Lane and I didn't manage to cover the history or even provide many answers, but we at least posed most of the questions.

How much of what is dumped into the "negative advertising" file folder really meets the definition? Shouldn't it be limited to untruths and half-truths that play to base emotions? Isn't there a need for calling out candidates, especially incumbents, for how they've acted and voted in the past? What's over the line? Do negative ads even work? If not, why are they so central to most American political campaigns? Is there a remedy to counter untruths, half-truths and misrepresentations?

The Myths of Negative Campaigning

The 1964 "Daisy" ad that began the program is legendary—a little girl counting petals she plucks off a daisy before her voice is replaced by the countdown of a rocket launch. The screen is then filled with the mushroom cloud and roar of a nuclear detonation. Barry Goldwater, the Republican presidential nominee, didn't even need to be named for the ad's creators to communicate that he wasn't to be trusted with the nation's nuclear arsenal.

The assumption behind negative campaigning is that it must work. Research is mixed, though. University of Washington professor David Domke said some researchers have found it can change voter behavior in limited circumstances, such as when the candidate delivering or benefiting from the negative message has favorable standing and the target does not. Other times it can drive down turnout.

Jeff Smith, the now-retired executive director of the Washington State Democratic Party, said he never saw a negative campaign that worked. It persists, he said, because consultants make money that way and party organizations feel pressure to look like they are doing something helpful.

What to do about it all? Nothing, probably. Laws against lying have been found unconstitutional. Fact-checkers in independent groups and the news media fight an uphill battle and are ignored by the campaigns themselves and their diehards. Which leaves voters as the enforcer. And since much research questions the effectiveness of negative campaigns, it might be that voters are already doing a pretty good job.

3

Negative Campaigning Undermines American Democracy

Todd Phillips

Todd Phillips is a political researcher and the founder of www .localelectors.org.

Negative campaigning is hurting America. It discourages good candidates from entering politics. Furthermore, it creates exaggerated and sometimes false messages about candidates and the efficacy of government. As a result, many Americans have lost faith in their political leaders. In addition, the process undermines the government's ability to address major challenges. It would be better to choose leaders like they do in business, where corporate executives break up responsibilities and delegate them to managers throughout the organization. The US electoral system needs to be reformed along those lines, with an emphasis on more community involvement and greater accountability.

Negative political campaigning has long been a staple of American politics, and now, with the advent of Super PACs [political action committees], it is being taken to a whole new level. According to *The Washington Post*, as of May 20 [2012], campaign spending by candidates and Super PACs had already totaled $138.6 million, and 68 percent of that has been negative.

Astounding Levels of Spending

Mitt Romney demonstrated during the primary that he was quite willing to use negative advertising to pummel his opponents. According to *The Washington Post*, 77 percent (down from 91 percent in late April) of the spending by Romney's Super PAC "Restore Our Future," or just over $27 million, has been used on negative advertising. The Romney campaign itself has spent $7.6 million, or 54 percent of its total, on negative advertising.

Four other Republican-leaning Super PACs have spent a combined $36.9 million on advertising, with 100 percent of their spending being negative.

President Obama's Super PAC "Priorities USA Action," by contrast, has spent $1.4 million, or 69 percent of its total, on negative advertising. The Obama campaign itself has spent $2.7 million, or 21 percent of its total, on negative advertising. Both campaigns will undoubtedly spend many more millions on negative advertising during the general election campaign.

Mitt Romney has also used personal appearances as opportunities to tear down the Obama administration. Just before launching his campaign in May 2011, he said on the *Today* show that Obama has "been one of the most ineffective presidents at the job at hand that I've ever seen." He later followed that up by saying that Obama's presidency has "failed." Ever since then, Mitt Romney has been unrelenting with this and similar messages.

U.S. House Speaker John Boehner had a similarly damning message during a recent appearance on Fox News, when he said, "America can't live for four more years with Barack Obama as president. His policies will turn America in a direction that we may never recover from." Negative messages such as this have been coming from Republicans ever since President Obama took office.

Assessing the Problem

Is all of this negativity a problem?

When candidates use negative advertising, we see it as unfair. They are competing not by trumpeting their own merits but by undermining their competition. And if one candidate has more money than his competition, as Mitt Romney did during the primaries, it just doesn't seem right. It feels like cheating.

As anyone involved in marketing or advertising knows, with repeated exposure, people tend to accept a message as fact.

It is also very unbecoming of candidates for high office to be negative. Imagine a candidate for the job of CEO at a major American corporation trying to undermine other candidates during the interview process. It would be unthinkable. Everyone knows that one of the cardinal rules of interviewing is to be positive. We associate negativity with failure and incompetence rather than with building, leading, and inspiring. And when someone is negative, there can be little doubt that he will be very difficult to work with, and a nightmare to work for. Being negative and being a leader are simply incompatible.

But the problems with negative campaigning run much deeper.

As anyone involved in marketing or advertising knows, with repeated exposure, people tend to accept a message as fact. In the 2012 presidential campaign, Mitt Romney's strategy, and the Republican strategy in general, has been to take advantage of this by bashing President Obama relentlessly ever since he took office. The American people have been exposed to a continuous stream of messages saying that "Obama is a bad guy," "Obama is a horrible president," and "Obama is a failure." According to *The Washington Post*, during this election cycle $66.9 million has been spent so far on ads with an "Anti-Obama Message." Naturally, over time many people will come to believe that Obama is indeed a failure. Since most people have no first-hand knowledge of his actions, it is hard to imagine how it could be otherwise.

The Scope of Negative Campaigning

Of course, negative campaigning isn't isolated to this campaign, or to the race for president in general; it's common in political campaigns across America. We are bombarded with messages telling us that candidates, politicians, and even the government are corrupt, incompetent failures. Candidates say this about their competitors, politicians say it about the opposing party, and special-interest groups pour money into Super PACs that run advertisements saying it about any politician opposing their agenda. Candidates seeking elected office for the first time almost universally justify their own election by saying the existing government is broken and that change is needed. Messages damning our government are practically beaten into us.

Negative campaigning prevents many good candidates from entering politics and leaves us with candidates who are comfortable with conflict. Government becomes populated with people who are primed for conflict, which causes deadlocks and paralysis, making the government less able to do the work of the people. This in turn leads to less support by the public, more negative campaigning, and fewer good candidates. It is a spiral of destruction.

Elections have become events where billions of dollars are spent bludgeoning the government and the people in it and undermining its legitimacy. Is it any surprise that opinion polls consistently show that Americans have little confidence in the government or in the people running it? Is it any wonder that bashing the government has become a favorite national pastime?

This is an extremely serious problem. How can a government be effective if it doesn't have the support of the people? How can our country be successful if our government is undermined? How can you or I be successful in a weak country?

Why do politicians engage in negative campaigning?

As political scientists Stephen Ansolabehere and Shanto Iyengar wrote in their book *Going Negative,* "voters tend to be risk-averse and prefer candidates who are perceived to have fewer negative attributes." It is much easier for a candidate to create doubts about his opponent than it is for him to prove his own self-worth. Negative campaigns are often targeted at an opponent's likely supporters in an attempt to embitter them toward the candidate so that they don't turn out to vote. In cases where small changes in turnout can affect the outcome of the election, this strategy can be very effective.

When we are uninformed and have no first-hand knowledge about something, we are easily influenced.

The Efficacy of Negative Campaigning

Why does negative campaigning work?

Surveys have consistently found that most people know very little about politics. Only about two thirds of people surveyed can name their state's governor. About half know that there are two U.S. senators from their state, and less than half can name their congressman/woman. And only about one in 10 people knows how their congressman/woman voted on any particular bill.

If people know so little about these critical, high-level facts, their detailed knowledge about candidates must be near zero!

When we are uninformed and have no first-hand knowledge about something, we are easily influenced.

Mitt Romney can call President Obama a failure because he knows that few people know the facts or can make an informed judgment themselves. He, and whoever else wants to influence elections and the government, can say almost whatever they want and most people have no way of knowing otherwise. Americans are sitting ducks for political propaganda.

To understand why this is a problem, it helps to put things into perspective.

Politics vs. Business

Consider the process successful businesses use when hiring new executives. They conduct multiple interviews and engage in in-depth questioning, they often give candidates tests, and they speak with numerous references. It is a very rigorous process. This is what is necessary in order to truly understand candidates so that good hiring decisions can be made.

The process we use to hire government leaders in our "democracy" is the polar opposite of this. Only a tiny percentage of people vote in primary elections. Then, in general elections, millions of people, most of whom are politically uninformed, go to the polls and cast votes for a long list of candidates. Most people simply vote according to their preferred party, so they don't really make a choice at all.

Our system of democracy is the way it is not because anyone designed it that way, but because of a series of ill-considered, incremental reforms.

Our "democracy" assumes that every citizen will know an extraordinary amount about politics and candidates, and that everyone will vote—but they don't.

Could it be that our expectations for people are unrealistic? Could we all be victims of a poorly designed democratic system?

Could this be the root problem with our government, with all other problems in government and many in our society stemming from this?

Rethinking Democracy

The Framers of our Constitution never intended our democracy to operate the way that it does. They feared mass democracy and went to great lengths to avoid it when writing our Constitution. Our system of democracy is the way it is not because anyone designed it that way, but because of a series of ill-considered, incremental reforms.

Our country has grown and changed enormously since our Constitution was ratified, and we have learned an enormous amount about people, organizations, and government since then. Could it be that the time has come to rethink democracy once again?

Consider this: Businesses are our best model for organizing large numbers of people, because competitive pressures force them to be efficient.

In large corporations, CEOs don't try to manage all their employees themselves; rather, they break up responsibilities into manageable chunks and delegate them to managers. Managers are arranged in layers, creating a hierarchy that forms an organization. Everyone in the organization is accountable to a manager, and ultimately to the CEO. The CEO is able to achieve business goals by working through a small number of top managers, thereby managing the entire organization. Corporations can consist of millions of people and be successful because they are organized this way.

Our country consists of millions of people, and it is clearly impractical for each citizen to be responsible for hiring and managing each of their representatives themselves. Might democracy work better if citizens delegated their political responsibilities more effectively so that democracy could operate like an organization?

A New System

This would mean that citizens, rather than electing a wide range of representatives for various offices, would only elect a single representative that is close to them, and delegate all political responsibility to that representative. This representative, along with all other representatives or office holders, would then be placed in a hierarchy, with each level in the hierarchy being elected/hired by the level below it. Citizens would be linked to the government via a chain of connected representatives.

People [should] not be given the unrealistic responsibility of being informed about numerous candidates, numerous issues, and the actions of a distant government, just as the CEO of a corporation is not responsible for personally managing every employee in the corporation.

This would require small election districts, which we will call communities. Citizens would be members of a community, and the representative they elect would be their community representative. In small communities, people would be able to know their representative personally, make good voting decisions, and hold their representative accountable for the results he or she produces throughout his or her term in office. With similarly small ratios throughout the hierarchy, representatives at each level could be held accountable by the level below them, and ultimately by the people.

People would participate in democracy primarily by participating in community meetings. They could present issues they are concerned about, and issues that are supported by the community would be pursued at the next level of government by their community representative. This process would be repeated at each level, and issues that are supported would rise to the top and become policy. This would allow citizens to set the agenda of all representatives and hold them accountable for the results they produce, much like a CEO does in a business. Such a process would allow people to manage the government.

With all elections taking place in small groups of connected people, there would be no place for negativity or propaganda, for the same reasons that there is no place for these things in a business. Candidates would likely already be known to everyone in the group, creating an ideal hiring situation. In addition, people would not be given the unrealistic responsibility of being informed about numerous candidates, numerous issues, and the actions of a distant government, just as the CEO of a corporation is not responsible for personally managing every employee in the corporation.

We have thought such a system of democracy through, and we believe that, because it addresses the root problem with democracy, it has the potential to eliminate all the problems in our government and many in our society. We call this system Local Electors, which is also the name we've given to the community representatives.

It is useful to remember something Albert Einstein once said: "The world we have created is a product of our thinking; it cannot be changed without changing our thinking."

4

Negative Campaigning Is Essential to Winning Elections

Andy Lewandowski

Andy Lewandowski is a Georgetown University graduate student and a contributor to Electronic Media & Politics.

It seems that Americans choose to believe in the myth of clean, fair elections devoid of negative campaigning. The reality is that political campaigns have always relied on negative campaigning because it is essential to winning. Candidates must chip away at their opponents' credibility and highlight the differences between them and their opponents. Dirty campaigns have been a staple of American politics for centuries, and it is important to remember that politics is a dirty, nasty business.

The 2012 U.S. presidential race is heating up as the Republican Party wrapped up its national convention last week [August 27–30, 2012] and the Democratic Party heads into its national convention this week [September 3–6, 2012]. With the conventions serving as both an official and symbolic start to the general election, the barrage of negative advertisements and attacks coming from both sides is seemingly growing stronger.

A Growing Concern

This presidential election cycle has seen a record amount of negativity that many in the news media as well as political circles have incessantly called out as antithetical to the democratic process. While much of the negativity can be traced back to the many attack ads seen on TV and the Internet, the news media are also fueling the general tone by emphasizing this negativity. Headlines have ranged from the exploratory, "Negative presidential campaign ads going to new extremes" and "New Week Brings More Negative Ads," to downright condemnation, "Voters Disgusted with Negative Ads" and "Too Negative: Voters Blast Obama, Romney Ads." And, in what is perhaps the most meta headline (and ad) of the bunch, the *Huffington Post* declared, "Mitt Romney Ad Attacks Obama For Negative Ads."

The Pew Research Center's Project for Excellence in Journalism provides evidence to the levels of negativity this election cycle has demonstrated. In a study released at the end of August, "The Master Character Narratives in Campaign 2012," Pew examined the "dominant or master narratives in the press about the character and record of presidential contenders." The study found that 72 percent of media coverage has been negative for Barack Obama and 71 percent has been negative for Mitt Romney. This is a substantial number for both candidates—and surprisingly equitable too, since both campaigns continue to condemn the other for negative campaign ads, when in fact both are fully engaged in producing attack ads. These numbers are considerably higher than 2008's, when a similar Pew study found negative media coverage to be a low 31 percent for Obama and 57 percent for John McCain.

Winning a presidential election is about chipping away at the credibility of one's opponent, which is made easier and quicker by going negative.

The news media are not only highlighting negative campaign ads and attacks, but [are] then going on to condemn the high levels of negativity seen this election cycle. (This may be indicative of a larger feedback loop phenomenon in American media and politics.) Where the negativity is coming from or which campaign is being more negative are not the questions. The real question is, so what? This isn't the first, nor is it the last, time politicians will engage in "dirty politics"—so why call foul?

Negative Campaigning As an Essential Tool

In June, *New York Magazine*'s Frank Rich wrote an essay about the merits of negative campaigning, calling it an essential part of winning. "The president, any president, should go negative early, often, and without apology if the goal is victory. The notion that negative campaigning is some toxic modern aberration in American democracy is bogus," he wrote. Rich goes on to trace the most negative and nasty campaigns in U.S. history, and to great aplomb. And he has a good point—going negative may very well be essential to winning a presidential election and should not be regarded as a failure of the American polity.

> *There remains a myth in American politics that going negative somehow betrays an electoral ideal of fair, clean play. But politics is inherently uneven and definitely dirty, and the U.S.'s greatest politicians have understood this well.*

Every four years, Americans circle back to a romanticized version of presidential campaigning, one where candidates point out each others' positive attributes and applaud each others' leadership. This fantasy version of campaigning never really plays out unless a candidate is winning political points for going positive, or staying "above the fray." As the news headlines have acutely pointed out, voters are "shocked" and "disgusted" by the levels of negativity in the 2012 election, even though the same electorate was just as shocked and disgusted by negativity four years ago, and eight years ago and so forth. The reality is that we hold our candidates and politicians to a higher level of integrity in rhetoric only. Winning a presidential election is about chipping away at the credibility of one's opponent, which is made easier and quicker by going negative. In this way, going negative is essential to winning, regardless of how voters feel about the practice.

The Benefits

There have been many academic studies that have highlighted the merits of going negative and explored possible effects on the electorate. Among these, [Paul] Freedman and [Kenneth] Goldstein (["Measuring Media Exposure and the Effects of Negative Campaign Ads," *American Journal of Political Science*] 1999) conducted a study that measured the effects of negative campaign ads. Their research was based on the then-existing notion that media exposure to negative ads depressed voter turnout. Surprisingly, their study found the exact opposite: exposure to negative ads actually increased the likelihood of voting by acting as a stimulator. Cited in their study, [Richard R.] Lau ([*An Analysis of US Senate Elections*] 1985) noted that there is "greater weight given to negative information relative to equally extreme and equally likely positive information."

Lau (1985) offered two explanations for the effects of going negative: the "figure-ground hypothesis" and the "cost-orientation hypothesis." The figure-ground hypothesis posits negative information "may be perpetually more salient, more easily noticed, and therefore more readily processed" than positive information. Put simply, negative ads stand out over positive ads, which may be why they have become a stalwart of sorts in presidential campaigns. Secondly, the cost-orientation hypothesis posits "people are more strongly motivated to avoid costs than to approach gains." In this way, voters are concerned about protecting their interests and avoiding risk, which are themes found in many negative ads. For example, various Obama ads have featured the charge that Romney will, if elected president, raise taxes on the middle-class. Based on Lau's hypothesis, it's easy to see how a viewer would take notice to such an accusation.

The Myth of Clean Elections

So why does going negative continue to get so much attention? There remains a myth in American politics that going negative somehow betrays an electoral ideal of fair, clean play. But politics is inherently uneven and definitely dirty, and the U.S.'s greatest politicians have understood this well. Their record of winning proves it. Our fear may simply lie in a betrayal of an intangible, American ideal. An ideal that is just that—something to aspire to and work toward, but one that rarely comes to fruition due to the campaign realities of running for president.

As Obama and Romney continue to duke it out this fall, it may be wise to remain cognizant of the fact that American elections have a long and storied history of nastiness and that negative campaigning is not unique to the 2012 election. This election's high levels of negativity could very well set a new modern-day precedent for presidential elections, or it could simply be a continuation of what's been a common circumstance in American politics since its founding. What's certain is that elections are about winning—and the campaign that understands this best will not pretend that going negative is a breach of the polity.

5

Political Mudslinging:
Does It Work?

Judy Beaupre

Judy Beaupre is a freelance writer and editor.

There was an unprecedented number of attack ads during the 2012 presidential primary. The main reason in the rising number of negative ads is the increasing political polarization of the electorate. For angry voters, negative ads play to their emotions and can motivate them to go to the polls. Another reason for the high number is the complicity of political journalists, who publicize nasty and juicy attack ads at the expense of substantive positive ads. Researchers have found that negative campaigning can be tricky: candidates must be careful to back up their outrageous claims or risk a backlash from both media and voters.

It's an image that, once seen, is hard to forget. A small, freckle-faced girl—the very embodiment of innocence—counting each petal that she removes from a daisy . . . her careful recitation soon drowned out by an ominous male voice counting backward to zero, her determined expression dissolving into a mushroom cloud that fills the screen. Run by the LBJ re-election campaign in 1964, it is often cited as the most famous attack ad in political history. Its intent: to play on voters' fear of nuclear war through an implicit suggestion that the hawkish stance of Johnson's Republican opponent, Barry Goldwater, would lead the country down a path of no return.

"The daisy ad was the first in the style of fear ad—it was an ad that was ahead of its time," says Ted Brader, associate professor of political science at the University of Michigan and the author of *Campaigning for Hearts and Minds: How Emotional Appeals in Political Ads Work*. "Campaign ads in the '50s, '60s, and '70s tended to rely more on jingles; they were not as hard-hitting as they are today."

Fast forward almost half a century, and negative advertising seems to be anything but the exception. Unlike the Johnson ad, which didn't mention Goldwater by name, today's campaign messaging is often explicit, calling out candidates on their views, their records, and even their character. John G. Geer, professor of political science at Vanderbilt University, has tracked political advertising since 1960, and has found a consistent upward trajectory in negativity. His most recent research shows that the proportion of negative political ads has increased from less than 10 percent in 1960 to more than 60 percent in 2008. It would seem that 2012 will top all previous records.

In recent decades, electronic and social media have drastically changed the channels through which voters gather information; media moguls have replaced the legions of local party workers once charged with informing and cajoling voters.

"In this year's Republican primary alone, we saw an unprecedented number of negative ads," said Dr. Geer. Three quarters of those run by Gingrich and Romney could be viewed as attack ads, in contrast to 1980, when Ronald Reagan didn't run a single negative ad in his bid for the Republican nomination, he said.

Despite these ebbs and swells—which largely reflect the evolution of political advertising since television became the medium of choice—the inflammatory tone of electoral confrontation is nothing new. Thomas Jefferson was derided as the anti-Christ, and Abraham Lincoln was lambasted as an idiot and a buffoon, allegations that make charges of flip-flopping and using a Swiss bank account for personal savings pale in comparison.

In recent decades, electronic and social media have drastically changed the channels through which voters gather information; media moguls have replaced the legions of local party workers once charged with informing and cajoling voters. During the past half century, as the first televised presidential debate captured our attention in 1960 and politicians began to feel their way through the boundless opportunities that television and, more recently, the Internet had to offer, the electoral tug-of-war has experienced a gradual but seismic shift in tone. What is it about the past few decades that has put candidates so firmly on the offensive, replacing reasoned debate with hostility, accusations, and occasional innuendos? Dr. Geer points to a widening ideological divide and what he calls "the Karl Rove hypothesis" that are to blame for candidates' incessant lashing out at one another.

"There are those who say that the ads themselves generate negativity, but I think that's borderline crazy," he says. "Instead I believe that it's our increased polarization that drives negativity. And consultants like Karl Rove and Mark Hanna have learned how to be more effective in their messaging." But Dr. Geer also points a finger at the media, charging that journalists share the blame, and that ads brimming with juicy accusations are more likely to find their way onto the evening news than a candidate's campaign promises.

Dr. Brader, whose 2006 book explored the use of emotion and the impact of music and visual imagery in political advertising, believes that negative ads have an important role to play in contemporary campaigns.

"Fear ads get a bad rap. They're seen by many as sinister, but in fact fear ads are not unsavory," he says. "They break people out of their political habits and make them pay attention to what's going on around them." He explains that when attention is focused on a potential danger—as in the daisy ad—voters engage in a more effortful process of gathering information that can inform their choices in the polls. "When there's nothing to fear, there's no reason to weigh the costs and benefits of a particular decision. It's easier to stick to the habits you already have," he says.

Although the daisy television ad aired only once, it cemented its place in political advertising history. In his "Attack Ad Hall of Fame," which grew from the research he did for his book *In Defense of Negativity: Attack Ads in Presidential Campaigns*, Dr. Geer identifies it as the best-known attack ad of all time. Its use of grainy black and white imagery and the unsettling contrast of background sounds—the child's voice amid chirping birds, abruptly overtaken by an earsplitting explosion and a booming male voice—put it at the forefront of fear-inducing, emotionally wrenching ads.

Targeting Emotions

The use of sound and imagery to shape voters' feelings—and ultimately the choices they make on election day—has been the focus of much of Dr. Brader's research. He has found that the influence of such auditory and visual impressions is often more important than the actual message itself.

> *Voters have long bemoaned the use of political tactics that they view as manipulative, unethical, dishonest, or sometimes salacious, but campaign strategists and psychologists agree that . . . these ads often work.*

"Emotions are ingrained at a biological level, and the use of imagery and music are a source of emotional power," he says. "Unlike words, which are used to inform or explain, images are purely for emotional impact. They are conduits to emotional reaction. We tend to react quickly to them."

The images and audio chosen to support a candidate's message can dramatically change the way in which it is received, Dr. Brader says. Repetitive noises, such as a ticking clock or beating heart, produce anxiety and tension, whereas images of a happy family or a waving flag can produce very different kinds of emotion.

Voters have long bemoaned the use of political tactics that they view as manipulative, unethical, dishonest, or sometimes salacious, but campaign strategists and psychologists agree that, despite the distaste they cause, these ads often work.

Although the earliest empirical research into the impact of attack ads—undertaken by UCLA's Stephen Ansolabehere and Shanto Iyengar in the mid-1990s—suggested that such negativity depressed voter turnout, instilling paralyzing apathy and keeping people home from the polls, recent studies have shown voters to be more resilient to negative messaging than originally thought. Attack ads tend to contain more substantive information than their positive counterparts, riveting the attention of voters and drawing clearer distinctions between candidates.

"To be fully informed, a voter needs to know the good and the bad," Dr. Geer says. "Candidates are good at telling you why you should vote for them, but not so good at telling you why you might not want to."

But unlike positive ads, which can create a "feel-good" tenor without much attention to specifics, he cautions that the demands of negativity are great. "You need to document what you're saying. You just can't make that stuff up. You're not going to accuse Mitt Romney of being stupid, for example, but you could say that about Sarah Palin since she let us know that she didn't know the difference between North and South Korea." Campaign strategists understand this demand; Dr.

Geer's research shows that 80 percent of negative ads include documentation, while only 20 percent of positive ads do.

Some attack ads take an entirely different approach, however. One particularly insidious type of messaging—sometimes referred to as stealth advertising—purports to convey one message while subtly sending a second, more-negative, and usually more-controversial message.

Like fear, anger can be a powerful motivator in political messaging.

In 1988, an independent political action committee supporting George H.W. Bush ran a television spot criticizing Bush's Democratic opponent, Michael Dukakis, for being "soft on crime." Well known in political circles as the infamous Willie Horton ad, the message focused on the story of convicted killer William Horton who—during Dukakis' term as Massachusetts governor—had been released on an unsupervised weekend pass, only to rape and kill again. While Bush's stand in favor of capital punishment came through loud and clear in the ad, so too did the less-than-subtle race card that the ad's creators deftly played. Using what looked like a prison mug shot that showed a dark-skinned African-American, they racialized his name (there is no record of Horton ever having been called Willie) and used stark colors and imagery to create frightening emotional overtones.

"The Willie Horton ad was well attuned to the primate brain, and particularly to the amygdala, which is highly responsive to both facial expressions and fear-evoking stimuli," says Emory University psychology professor Drew Westen in his book, *The Political Brain.* "The ad was packed with both. The mug shot of Horton . . . [played] on every white person's fears of the dangerous, lawless, violent, dark black male. Research shows that even subliminal presentation of black faces activates the amygdala in whites, and implicit racial appeals are more effective than explicit ones because they don't raise people's conscious attitudes toward racism."

Anger as a Motivator

Like fear, anger can be a powerful motivator in political messaging.

"Anger energizes us to do something," says Dr. Brader. "When we're angry, we're not particularly open-minded. What we experience is an unpleasant emotion that comes in response to obstacles we encounter—usually something that we perceive as undeserved or unjust." But anger can be a tricky emotion to evoke, because it works two ways. While a carefully orchestrated message may be successful in enraging and further galvanizing a candidate's supporters, it is likely to produce similar fury—but for different reasons—in the opponent's camp.

The real question though—for both politicians and psychologists—is the effect that such negativity has on voter behavior and, ultimately, on election outcomes.

He offers as evidence a 30-second commercial that Republican Jesse Helms ran against his Democratic opponent Harvey Gantt in a 1990 North Carolina Senate race. The brief video clip showed a pair of Caucasian hands opening and then crumpling an employment rejection letter while the voiceover lambasted Gantt's support of an affirmative action quota system that set aside jobs for "less qualified" minority job seekers.

"It was classic in its effectiveness in producing anger for both sides," Dr. Brader says. "For Helms, it was about blaming someone else for what happened to you. But Democrats were angry at the cynical implication of race as the problem."

The real question though—for both politicians and psychologists—is the effect that such negativity has on voter behavior and, ultimately, on election outcomes. Dr. Geer suggests that, while such ads can get voters to the polls and help clarify their balloting decisions, it's often a toss-up as to whether they are actually more effective in achieving their purpose than positive ads. His research shows that messages aimed at building enthusiasm for a candidate—typically the incumbent—can generate a small bump in voter turnout and support, while negative ads are typically credited with a greater effect.

"There's always a risk with negative advertising, though," he says. "If you don't have the evidence to back up your claim, it can come back to haunt you. So the range of effect in negative advertising is broader; it can result in a big positive bump or a big negative effect."

In 2008, John McCain ran a commercial charging Barack Obama with planning to teach sex education to kindergartners. "It wasn't true and got him immediate pushback," Dr. Geer says. The ad was pulled, and McCain's popularity took a hit as a result.

Dr. Brader has also noted the effectiveness of negative ads. For his book, Dr. Brader tracked short-term reactions of viewers, who were questioned—shortly after seeing political ads—about how their attitudes toward candidates were affected, who they thought they would vote for, and how willing they were to show up to vote. Generally speaking, negative ads did seem to work, and there was evidence that they were particularly effective in increasing the attention that voters paid to specific issues. Timing and placement of the ads proved critical; Dr. Brader's team reported that when political commercials were aired during a news program, viewers expressed more interest in news segments about the same issue.

For voters still trying to make or clarify their balloting decisions, this year is likely to be the most challenging of all. There is a new and powerful player in the 2012 round of electoral wrangling, a wild card that may do more than shatter all previous campaign advertising records—both in terms of dollars spent and vitriol levied: the SuperPAC.

These independently financed political action committees—blessed by the Supreme Court and accountable to no one—have the virtually unlimited ability to launch undocumented attacks against the opposition. According to the Annenberg Public Policy Center, some $41 million was spent by SuperPACs during the Republican primary contest alone, and more than half of that—a total of $23.3 million—went toward "ads that included deceptive or misleading claims." Only time will tell what the final price tag or the eventual outcome of the Obama-Romney contest will be.

"I think it's safe to say that most SuperPAC ads will be negative," says Dr. Geer. "It will be interesting to watch—the candidates may decide to run only positive ads and let the SuperPACs do the dirty work. We'll have to wait and see, but it could change the tone of much of the official campaign messaging."

6

Fact-Checking Does Not Stop Negative Campaigning

David Corn

David Corn is an author, political commentator, journalist, and the chief of the Washington bureau for Mother Jones *magazine.*

The fact-checking of political campaigns has been on the rise since the early years of the 2000s when news organizations failed to vet the George W. Bush administration's evidence for the Iraq War properly. In response, a number of fact-checking organizations have been created to rate the accuracy of campaign statements and political ads. However, a number of political campaigns have ignored the claims of fact-checkers and have continued to put out exaggerated attack ads and make false campaign statements. For these politicians, lying can still land a significant blow and damage an opponent—even if they take a hit themselves.

As Mitt Romney was buttoning up the Republican nomination this past spring, he addressed the annual convention of the American Society of News Editors in the cavernous ballroom of the Marriott Wardman Park hotel in Washington, DC. He blasted President Obama for breaking a "promise" to keep unemployment below 8 percent—a charge that had previously earned Romney three Pinocchios from the *Washington Post*'s "Fact Checker" column. He also slammed the president for "apologizing for America abroad"—an accusation that

David Corn, "How to Beat the Fact-Checkers," *Mother Jones*, September–October 2012. © 2012, Foundation for National Progress. All rights reserved. Reproduced by permission.

PolitiFact had months earlier branded a "pants on fire" lie. And he accused Obama of adding "nearly as much public debt as all the prior presidents combined" (a statement already judged "an exaggeration" by *FactCheck.org*) and of cutting $500 million from Medicare (a "false" assertion according to *PolitiFact*).

A politician mangling the truth is hardly news. Yet what was notable about this moment was that the candidate felt no compunction about appearing before more than 1,500 journalists and repeating whoppers that their own colleagues had so roundly debunked. Nor was Romney challenged about any of these untruths when it came time to ask questions. He was able to peddle a string of officially determined falsehoods before a crowd of newspaper editors—repeat: *a crowd of newspaper editors*—and face absolutely no consequences. The uncomfortable question for the press: With the news cycle overwhelmed by the headline-of-the-nanosecond, and with politicians ignoring or openly challenging the truth cops, how much does the much-heralded political fact-checking industry really matter?

The politicians will twist or spin information if they believe it will advance their political interests.

The Rise of Fact-Checking in Politics

Big Media's push for independent and ongoing verification of newsmakers' statements stretches back to the mid-2000s, when many news organizations were on the defensive over their failure to vet the Bush administration's claims about weapons of mass destruction in Iraq. The Annenberg Public Policy Center at the University of Pennsylvania launched *FactCheck.org*, with veteran CNN reporter Brooks Jackson at the helm, in 2003. *PolitiFact*, created by the *St. Petersburg Times*, and the *Washington Post*'s Fact Checker followed four years later.

At the *Post*, reporter Michael Dobbs had proposed creating the Fact Checker feature because he believed, as he put it in a New America Foundation report, DC reporting had "strayed away from the truth-seeking tradition" and become too hung up on the "he said, she said aspect." Dobbs, who as a member of the paper's national security team had seen what he called the "weapons of factual destruction" up close, said journalists were "permitting presidential candidates and others to get away with sometimes outrageous falsehoods."

On the face of it, the fact-checking shops have thrived. Glenn Kessler, who inherited the *Post* column from Dobbs, now draws about 1 million page views a month, *PolitiFact* has set up sites in 11 states to zero in on local pols; it employs 35 full-time journalists. *FactCheck.org* has inspired *FlackCheck.org*, which uses humor to debunk spin. But as these operations expand in profile and size, are politicians any less inclined to distort and dissemble?

"I'm often asked this," Kessler says, "and my response is, 'I don't write for the politicians. I write for the voters.' The politicians will twist or spin information if they believe it will advance their political interests. With Romney, for instance, no matter how many times we say it is not true that Barack Obama apologized for America, he will not change that line. For his political interests, it's a good line."

The Impact

Not all politicians, Kessler notes, have been so nonchalant. Back during the 2000 campaign, when he was fact-checking the presidential debates for the *Post*, Al Gore campaign aides "freaked out," anxiously calling him ahead of debates to explain the facts that Gore intended to deploy—and making changes in response to his objections. (At the time, Gore was fighting the charge that he was a serial fabricator.) The Bush campaign, by contrast, couldn't have cared less about the fact-checking push. Ari Fleischer, Bush's press secretary, "laughed about it," Kessler recalls.

On Capitol Hill, too, some members have shown more respect for the fact-checkers than others. A senior Republican once told Kessler that he had closely reviewed his columns on health care to ensure he would not repeat claims judged false. In response to a controversial *PolitiFact* ruling blasting Democrats for claiming that the Republican House budget would end Medicare—rather than end it "as we know it"—Sen. Sherrod Brown (D-Ohio) changed how he referred to the GOP plan. Media fact-checking, Brown once said publicly, "makes us a little more cautious about what we repeat that we've heard." (That same Medicare ruling, though, fueled a high-octane feud between *PolitiFact* and MSNBC's Rachel Maddow, who attacked the fact-checkers' conclusion as a product of GOP spin and declared *PolitiFact* "irrelevant.")

Brown's appreciation for fact-checking may be heightened because he is in a tough campaign against state Treasurer Josh Mandel, a Republican who has racked up a series of poor ratings from *PolitiFact*, including a "pants on fire" for calling Brown "one of the main DC politicians responsible for Ohio jobs moving to China." Mandel responded to that rating not by changing his tune, but by going after the fact-checkers, insisting that not only was the claim "100 percent truth" but that he would repeat it "again and again."

The 2012 Campaign

And what of the 2012 presidential campaign? Have Obama and Romney been swayed by the work of the professional fact-checkers? Bill Adair, who runs *PolitiFact*, points to a few instances—just a few—when Obama shifted rhetorical direction in response to fact-check rulings. In 2008, he ceased saying that gas prices were "higher than ever" after *PolitiFact* reported that this was false when accounting for inflation. Later, when the president was pushing for health care reform, *PolitiFact* challenged his statement that consumers could keep their current plans under the new law. (Market upheaval, it contended, might knock out some existing insurance policies.) The president then tweaked his language, saying that nothing in the bill would *force* consumers to switch, but he has since relapsed and used the original formulation.

Asked for an example of Romney altering an assertion or ad in response to a fact-check, Adair, after a long pause, remarks, "I don't recall one offhand. . . . They have quoted us a lot—when it boosts their case."

Kessler says the rise of fact-checking has led to political marketers striving for "a modicum of truthiness" in their ads—such as including citations. But, he adds, that hardly means the spots are any more accurate. When he examined an ad produced by the Koch brothers' Americans for Prosperity that accused the president of spending billions of stimulus dollars for green-energy jobs "overseas," he found that the spot had blatantly misrepresented the news stories it cited. (Four Pinocchios!)

The Obama and Romney operations had each come to see the fact-checkers . . . not as arbiters whose verdicts must be heeded, but as participants in the ever-roiling political tussle.

Whether or not they change their tune in response to the fact-checkers, the Obama and Romney organizations do spend time tending to them. The Obama campaign has assigned a deputy press secretary to be its point person for fact-checkers' questions. Several staffers at Romney HQ do the same. Both campaigns complain about being overwhelmed by the requests that flood their inboxes, and they gripe about the ensuing judgments. "If we say the sky is blue, we would get a 'half-true' because we didn't give the full explanation that the sky is blue because of chemical reactions that occurred in the atmosphere a million years ago," one aide grouses.

The Bain Controversy

One major subplot of the summer campaign season began when the *Post*'s Fact Checker column handed the Obama campaign four Pinocchios for calling Romney a "corporate raider [who] shipped jobs to China and Mexico." The vetters argued that Bain Capital's investments in outsourcing firms came after Romney claimed he left the company in February 1999. Yet on the same day, a lengthy investigation by another *Post* reporter showed that Romney had invested in outsourcing firms well before that point. That set off a controversy over when exactly Romney left Bain: After I reported that Securities and Exchange Commission documents listed him as being involved well into 2001, other outlets picked up the story, and the Romney campaign was forced to argue that signing SEC filings and being listed as managing director, president, and CEO of the company did not mean he was involved with Bain deals in any way.

By this time, it was clear that the Obama and Romney operations had each come to see the fact-checkers the same way candidate Mandel did in Ohio: not as arbiters whose verdicts must be heeded, but as participants in the ever-roiling political tussle. The Obama campaign released a six-page letter challenging the fact-checkers' findings on the outsourcing claim, while the Romney campaign put out a TV spot that charged Obama with bending the truth, and demanded an apology.

In the end, the flood of vetting fosters the they-all-do-it impression that gives cover to pols who prevaricate the most.

The Danger of Partisanship

This is no small matter: If fact-checking comes to be seen as merely another front in routine political warfare, that perception threatens the whole enterprise. To judge credibility, the fact-checkers must be regarded as credible judges. But each time they are pulled into a scuffle with politicians, they can look more like political actors to the public—an assumption that especially benefits those politicians who lie with the greatest abandon.

That's particularly ironic because the fact-checkers go out of their way to not appear the least bit partisan—none of the three sites will offer a verdict on which candidate lies more, or with greater panache. "I try to avoid being quoted saying either side has more falsehoods than the other," Adair says. As of July, the *Post*'s Pinocchio tracker did show Obama with a slightly lower average number of Pinocchios than Romney—but this ranking was based only on the statements the column happened to review. (Michele Bachmann had the highest average for the 2012 primary campaign.) That same month, *Politi-Fact* noted that of the Romney statements it had examined, 31 percent were true or mostly true, 17 percent were false, and 13 percent had earned a "pants on fire." Obama fared better, with 46 percent of his claims rated true or mostly true, 15 percent false, and only 5 percent "pants on fire."

But with the fact-checking outfits knocking both candidates and declining to explicitly compare their relative slipperiness, it might actually be easier for politicians to weather Pinocchios, pants-on-fire ratings, and whatnot. In the end, the flood of vetting fosters the they-all-do-it impression that gives cover to pols who prevaricate the most. One might argue that, say, Romney's untruths have been more foundational than Obama's (such as when he asserted there had been "no new jobs" created under Obama), but with all the Pinocchios flying about, such a distinction can be lost. The major incentive for lying—to score a political point—remains unchanged.

An "Elite Specialization"

That's in part because fact-checking has remained its own ghetto—or, as Adair prefers to call it, an "elite specialization."

"I am a supplement to political coverage, not a replacement," Kessler says. "I can go on for 2,000 words to examine one phrase. It's hard to do that on a daily story." And unlike the beat reporters, adds Adair, he and his team don't have to fret about maintaining access to campaign sources. Day-to-day reporting, by contrast, remains focused on the who's up/who's down, gaffe-du-jour, rubber-and-glue game of the campaign trail. This summer, I suggested to a well-regarded reporter covering Romney that it might be worth asking the candidate about a particularly bogus claim he had been making: "With Obamacare fully installed, government will come to control half the economy, and we will have effectively ceased to be a free-enterprise society." I had written about the charge—quoting one economist who called it "ridiculous" and another who said, "This analysis is so stupid it is hard to know where to begin"—and *FactCheck.org* subsequently dubbed it "patently false and misleading," while Kessler handed it four Pinocchios.

But the reporter, caught up in the spectacle of Romney's latest bus tour, hadn't heard of the remark, nor any of the vetting. With the news cycle moving at Twitter speed, a candidate snared in a lie only has to wait a few moments for the media to move on. The sting fades quickly.

In the weeks following my conversation with the reporter, Romney did not repeat his outlandish claim. Had the fact-checkers derailed the charge? There was no telling. But after the Supreme Court upheld the constitutionality of Obamacare, his campaign released a statement from a surrogate noting that Obama favored a "government-centered society" with "government-rationed healthcare." *FactCheck.org* and *PolitiFact* had each previously stated that it was inaccurate to refer to Obamacare as rationing. The Romney camp didn't care.

But the campaign was paying close attention to the vetters in one way—as a convenient supply of ammunition. When it zapped out a press release accusing Obama of hurling "dis-

credited distortions" about Romney's Bain record, it promi-
nently noted its sources: Kessler and *FactCheck.org*.

7

Social Media Does Not Act as a Check on Negative Campaigning

Caleb Garling

Caleb Garling is a San Francisco Chronicle *staff writer.*

Experts believe that social media did not have a significant impact on the 2012 US presidential election. In particular, social media largely failed to stop the spread of negative campaigning. One reason for this is that Americans are increasingly using social media in partisan ways—connecting to like-minded people and disconnecting from those with different political views. Campaigns knew that they could exaggerate or lie with little blowback from social media because there is little meaningful cross-talk between different ideological groups. Political candidates utilized social media as a campaign tool: soliciting money, collecting volunteers, motivating supporters, and putting out campaign ads and messages.

When President Obama used Twitter as his first communication medium to claim re-election Tuesday [November 6, 2012], the tweet became the most amplified message the service had ever seen.

It was the culminating moment in an election in which the role of the Internet was a constant, sometimes deafening, presence. CNN broadcast with on-screen hashtags—a way of linking tweets. Obama and his Republican challenger Mitt Romney boasted 33 million and 12 million Facebook fans, respectively. Countless election "memes"—digital snippets of pop culture—propagated on media sites like YouTube and Tumblr. The president even took time to have a question-and-answer session on ultra-geek social network Reddit.

What isn't clear days later—besides the final results in Florida—is the extent to which our growing digital connectivity actually affected the election's outcome. For all the incessant tweeting, posting, commenting and live-blogging across the Internet, did it ultimately change anything?

Polling outfit Pew Research published a study on the day of the election entitled "Social Media and Voting" that found that 22 percent of registered voters told friends and followers how they voted on sites such as Facebook or Twitter. But those conversations might just as well have happened elsewhere, and, more importantly, might have had different outcomes.

Fighting Words

While the Internet overflows with information—true and otherwise—both liberal and conservative Americans are increasingly homogeneous in the way they access it, argues Michael Heaney, a political science professor at the University of Michigan. The December issue of *American Behavioral Scientist* will feature a paper in which he argues this trend is spreading further into offline activities as well.

"Social media helps to reinforce the already strong tendency toward polarization—and worsens those trends in the electorate," he says. "People search out these little groups where everyone agrees with them," rather than engaging in authentic debate.

A March poll from Pew reinforces Heaney's observation. The study found that 9 percent of social-network users have gone so far as to block or "unfriend" someone who posted a disagreeable political opinion. Conversely, the study also reported that a fifth of users don't talk about their politics for fear of offending others.

Clearly, digital connectivity during the election did have important benefits.

Internet companies reflect this trend back onto the electorate. Microsoft went so far as to tweak its Bing search engine to give users an option to "customize" their political news by selecting "left," "right" or "center." Search engines like Google look at past search histories and revise future results to better suit what it determines the user wants to find. Repeatedly searching for "Barack Obama" returns more sites relevant to Obama in the future.

This does not mean Google is politically biased, says Danny Sullivan, editor of Search Engine Land, a website that tracks search technologies; it's just a product of the way the software works.

"Every search engine has biases that are a natural consequence of trying to rank web pages based on a wide range of factors," he wrote recently. "But by no means are these results somehow doing something favorable for Obama over Romney."

Clearly, digital connectivity during the election did have important benefits. Issues arising at polling stations were immediately made public. New Jersey voters could easily monitor their state's altered procedures in the wake of Superstorm Sandy. There were countless resources to help voters register and find polling places. Being able to check e-mail, text, read and watch movies on a smartphone no doubt kept some voters in long lines when they might otherwise have gone home out of boredom or impatience.

And digital resources served to check the veracity of political claims. Organizations like FactCheck.org at the University of Pennsylvania or Pulitzer Prize-winning Politifact parse the rhetoric and shed light on the truth. News aggregating sites like AllSides try to capture the entirety of a political story by doing side-by-side comparisons of stories from across the political spectrum.

False Information

But with online discourse so heavily siloed, these watchdogs' efforts can go for naught. Heaney believes the 2012 presidential campaigns generated the most false information ever—but the campaigns knew they could get away with it.

"This strategy only works if there is no meaningful crosstalk," he says.

The Internet also magnified supposed campaign "turning points." Much was made, for instance, of the presidential debates, especially of Obama's lackluster performance in the first one.

However, the political projection site Electoral Vote— which aggregates data from pollsters like Rasmussen and Gallup—predicted Obama would win the election with 332 Electoral College votes on Oct. 3—the day before the first debate. More than a month and three debates later, that appears to be precisely the number of votes the president will carry.

Business Entities

There are factors at play on the other side of the Internet curtain. The public tends to view social networks like YouTube, Facebook and Twitter as free services and public forums. But these organizations are, in fact, businesses—many of which have to answer to the demands of Wall Street. Jason Benlevi, a tech marketing veteran and the author of *Too Much Magic*, a book critical of cyber-utopian visions of the Internet as a panacea, says he still believes in technology as a societal solution.

"I just don't believe in the people pushing it," he says.

It's in the business interest of social networks and most websites to keep us talking and bantering back and forth. Revenue and data come from not only increasing the number of users, but users' engagement with friends and followers. Online businesses tinker with mathematical representations of the way people influence each other—sometimes called "social graphs"—and leverage them to achieve both goals.

In turn, they use the information to sell advertisements or additional services. These proprietary calculations are well guarded so it's difficult to say how much of their interest is vested in users branching out from their own political views.

Campaign Tool

The presidential campaigns used similar strategies when pushing their candidates to the public, and used social media as a listening tool.

With each passing election, social media are becoming less novel—another tool alongside TV ads and door-to-door canvassing.

Software company Evidon shines a light on the Web's monitoring tools with a piece of browser software called Ghostery. When a user goes to a new Web page, Ghostery examines all the third-party pieces of software that are registering metrics like clicks or the amount of time someone stays on a particular page. Myriad companies, from Google to Doubleclick, build and sell tools for companies to get a better picture of who is visiting their sites—and serve up better advertisements.

But campaigns can use them, too. From May to September, Ghostery users experienced 87 different tracking technologies on BarackObama.com; MittRomney.com had 48. Most of the tracking devices were ad-related software, notes Andy Kahl, consumer products director at Evidon. The candidates weren't serving up ads, however, but using the ad-targeting software to present relevant or new campaign messaging.

With each passing election, social media are becoming less novel—another tool alongside TV ads and door-to-door canvassing. In 2008, the Obama campaign honed its Twitter and Facebook use for fundraising and to drum up support, especially from younger voters, as the John McCain troops struggled to catch up. Though Romney used them far less than Obama in the 2012 campaign—perhaps a reflection of his campaign's target electorate—tweets and Facebook updates were still commonplace.

Superficial Dialogue

Micah Sifry, director of Personal Democracy Media and professor at Harvard's Kennedy School of Government, doesn't believe that any of the digital outlets—from Tumblr and Instagram to Facebook "townhalls" and Google "hangouts"—had any noticeable effect on the course of the election. He says they did little beyond foster the often superficial dialogue.

"Both sides benefited: The politicians got a little 'Internet buzz' for their appearances, and the tech companies got some welcome and cheap marketing," he wrote on election day. "And with a few exceptions, the political reporters who cover the election campaigns went merrily along for the ride."

8

The *Citizens United* Decision Will Increase Negative Political Ads

John Nichols and Robert W. McChesney

John Nichols is a journalist, author, and the Washington corre-spondent for The Nation. *Robert W. McChesney is an author, journalist, and professor at the University of Illinois at Urbana-Champaign.*

The US Supreme Court 2010 decision in Citizens United v. Fed-eral Election Commission *eased restrictions on corporate and individual spending on political campaigns and has led to the proliferation of Super PACs, or political action committees. Super PACs have become key players in local, state, and national elec-tions, allowing a range of contributors and groups to come to-gether on behalf of a candidate or issue. In the past few years, these groups have produced and aired a number of nasty and spurious attack ads. TV stations and other media outlets wel-come the windfall in revenue provided by Super PAC advertis-ing, and most news media do not have the will or the resources to fully investigate the sources of these ads. Many critics view Super PACs as a threat to democracy because they can inject large amounts of money into the political process with little ac-countability.*

We have seen the future of electoral politics flashing across the screens of local TV stations from Iowa to New Hampshire to South Carolina. Despite all the excitement about Facebook and Twitter, the critical election battles of 2012 and for some time to come will be fought in the commercial breaks on local network affiliates. This year, according to a fresh report to investors from Needham and Company's industry analysts, television stations will reap as much as $5 billion—up from $2.8 billion in 2008—from a money-and-media election complex that plays a definitional role in our political discourse. As Obama campaign adviser David Axelrod says, the cacophony of broadcast commercials remains "the nuclear weapon" of American politics.

We've known for some time that the pattern, extent and impact of political advertising would be transformed and supercharged by the Supreme Court's January 2010 *Citizens United* ruling. But the changes, even at this early stage of the 2012 campaign, have proven to be more dramatic and unsettling than all but the most fretful analysts had imagined.

A New Era

Citizens United's easing of restrictions on corporate and individual spending, especially by organizations not under the control of candidates, has led to the proliferation of "Super PACs [political action committees]." These shadowy groups do not have to abide by the $2,500 limit on donations to actual campaigns, and they can easily avoid rules for reporting sources of contributions. For instance, Super PACs have established nonprofit arms that are permitted to shield contributors' identities as long as they spend no more than 50 percent of their money on electoral politics. So the identity of many, possibly most, contributors will never be known to the public, even though they are already playing a decisive role in the 2012 election season. Former White House political czar Karl Rove's Crossroads complex, for example, operates both a Super PAC and a nonprofit. And Rove's operation is being replicated almost daily by new political operations aiming their money at presidential, Congressional, state and local elections. "In 2010, it was just training wheels, and those training wheels will come off in 2012," says Kenneth Goldstein, president of Kantar Media's Campaign Media Analysis Group. "There will be more, bigger groups spending, and not just on one side but on both sides."

The 2012 campaign has already confirmed that Super PACs are key players, more powerful in many ways than the campaigns waged by candidates and party committees. But don't expect commercial media outlets to shed much light on these secretive powers. Newsroom staffs have been cut, political reporting is down and local stations are too busy cashing in on what *TV Technology* magazine describes as "the political windfall." The *Citizens United* ruling and its Super PAC spawn have created a new revenue stream for media companies, and they are not about to turn the spigot off. "Voters are going to be inundated with more campaign advertising than ever," one investor service wrote in 2011. "While this may fray the already frazzled nerves of the American people, it is great news for media companies." Indeed, Super PAC ads allow stations to reap revenues from actual campaigns and from parallel "independent" campaigns targeting the same audience with different messages.

Who finished first in Iowa? And a week later in New Hampshire? The guy with the great hair and all the talk about "principles"—Mitt Romney.

Here's what the next stage of American politics looks like on the screen: WHO, the NBC affiliate in Des Moines, was awash in political advertising the night before the Iowa caucuses. But some ads stood out. One of the most striking was a minute-long commercial featuring amber waves of grain fluttering in the summer breeze, children smiling and a fellow with great hair declaring, "The principles that have made this nation a great and powerful leader of the world have not lost their meaning. They never will." Then the guy with the great hair announced, "I'm Mitt Romney. I believe in America. And I am running for president of the United States."

The Second Ad

Then came another ad, darker and more threatening, with grainy production values, old black-and-white photos and a blistering assault on the Republican presidential contender who had briefly leapt ahead of Romney in the polling: former House Speaker Newt Gingrich. "Newt has more baggage than the airlines," the ad warned, before linking Gingrich to "China's brutal one-child policy," "taxpayer funding of some abortions," "ethics violations" and "half-baked and not especially conservative ideals." Quoting a *National Review* poke at Gingrich, the ad closed with the line: "He appears unable to transform, or even govern, himself."

The first commercial is an old-school "closing argument" ad, all optimism and light, along with the usual campaign-season balderdash—the empty banalities of a front-running contender appealing to "principles" and a belief in America. The second represents another archetype: the no-holds-barred takedown of an opposing candidate, which politicians and their consultants traditionally avoid running on the eve of a big vote for fear of muddying their own message and appearing too negative. Romney's campaign paid for the "amber waves of grain" ad. But who was responsible for the "Newt Gingrich: Too Much Baggage" ad? Restore Our Future, a Super PAC that collected $30 million for the 2012 campaign—more than the combined spending of Lyndon Johnson and Barry Goldwater on the 1964 presidential campaign. And when Gingrich shot to the top of the polls a month before the Iowa caucuses, the group steered $4 million into a TV ad campaign that knocked the former Speaker out of the lead and into a dismal fourth-place finish.

Who finished first in Iowa? And a week later in New Hampshire? The guy with the great hair and all the talk about "principles"—Mitt Romney. He also happened to be the guy who appeared before a dozen potential donors at the organizational meeting for Restore Our Future in July 2011. Romney's former chief campaign fundraiser moved over to Restore Our Future, as well as his former political director and other aides. Romney's old partner at Bain Capital helped Restore Our Future get off the ground with a $1 million check. Technically there can be no collaboration between Super PACs and the candidates they are supporting. But Timothy Egan of the *New York Times* stated the obvious: "This legalism of 'no coordination' is a filament-thin G-string. Everyone coordinates."

Gingrich complained about the presumably unethical and potentially illegal level of coordination between the "principled" Romney campaign and the thuggish Restore Our Future project. When Romney pled innocence and ignorance, Gingrich said: "He's not truthful about his PAC, which has his staff running it and his millionaire friends donating to it, although in secret. And the PAC itself is not truthful in its ads." But the griping didn't get him very far.

The Explosion of Super PAC Money

By the time the 2012 race formally began, on January 3, Super PACs had already logged $13.1 million in campaign spending in early caucus and primary states, most of it in Iowa and most of it negative. Romney, whose actual campaign spent only about one-third as much money on ads as did the Super PACs that supported him, emerged as the narrow winner. But he wasn't the only winner in Iowa or New Hampshire, where a similar scenario played out a week later. Local television stations like WHO in Des Moines and WMUR in Manchester cashed in, big-time, as would stations in later primary states. And station managers in battleground states across the country can hardly wait for the real rush, which will come when the Super PACs that have already been positioned to support the Republican nominee and Democrat Barack Obama spend their money in what is all but certain to be the first multibillion-dollar presidential race in history.

For many stations, political advertising in 2012 could account for more than 20 percent of ad revenues, and in some key states far more than that.

The total number of TV ads for House, Senate and gubernatorial candidates in 2010 was 2,870,000. This was a 250 percent increase over the number of TV ads aired in 2002, when the same mix of federal and state offices was up for grabs. Compared strictly with 2008, the amount spent on TV ads for House races in 2010 was up 54 percent, and the amount spent on Senate-race TV ads was up 71 percent. Even before this year's Iowa binge, it was clear that 2012 would see a quantum leap in spending from 2008, the greatest increase in American history, and most of this would go to TV ads. As Maribeth Papuga, who oversees local TV and radio purchases for the Media Vest Communications Group, says, "We're definitely going to see a big bump in spending in 2012."

Changing Political Landscape

It's not as if Americans haven't already seen big bumps on what is becoming the permanent campaign trail. Consider how politics has changed in the past four decades. In 1972, a little-known Colorado Democrat, Floyd Haskell, spent $81,000 (roughly $440,000 in 2010 dollars) on television advertising for a campaign that unseated incumbent Republican US Senator Gordon Allott. The figure was dramatic enough to merit note in a *New York Times* article on Haskell's upset win. Fast-forward to the 2010 Senate race, when incumbent Colorado Democrat Michael Bennet defeated Republican Ken Buck. The total spent on that campaign in 2010 (the bulk of which went to television ads) topped $40 million, more than $30 million of which was spent by Super PAC-type groups answering only to their donors. In the last month of the election, negative ads ran nearly every minute of every day. The difference in spending, factoring in inflation, approached 100 to 1. The 2010 Colorado Senate race is generally held up by insiders as the bellwether for 2012 and beyond. As Tim Egan puts it, "This is your democracy on meth—the post-*Citizens United* world."

Super PAC advertising is not like traditional campaign advertising.

A Growing Revenue Stream

Local TV stations across the country have come to rely on the booms in political advertising that come during critical election contests. In the '70s, political ads were an almost imperceptible part of total TV ad revenues. By 1996, according to the National Association of Broadcasters (NAB), they had edged up to 1.2 percent. A decade later political advertising was approaching 8–10 percent of total TV ad revenue. For many stations, political advertising in 2012 could account for more than 20 percent of ad revenues, and in some key states far more than that. As former New Jersey Senator Bill Bradley put it, election campaigns "function as collection agencies for broadcasters. You simply transfer money from contributors to television stations."

The 2010 election season saw record spending on broadcast advertising: as much as $2.8 billion. And that wasn't even a presidential election year. Wall Street stock analysts can barely contain themselves as they envision the growing cash flow. Eric Greenberg, a veteran broadcast-industry insider, says, "Political advertising and elections are to TV what Christmas is to retail."

Broadcasters aren't about to give away the present they have received from the Supreme Court. The NAB has a long history of lobbying to block any campaign finance reform that would decrease revenues for local television stations, such as the idea of compelling stations to provide free airtime to candidates as a public-service requirement. The NAB's prowess in Washington was summed up by former Colorado Representative Pat Schroeder, who said, "Their lobbying is so effective, they hardly have to flick an eyelash." After the *Citizens United* ruling, the NAB actively opposed key provisions of the DISCLOSE Act, a measure supported by Congressional Democrats and a handful of reform-minded Republicans to roll back elements of the decision. But that's not all. The group has even opposed steps toward the transparency that Supreme Court justices who backed the *Citizens United* ruling agree is vital but that might shame (or at least expose) the excesses of Super PACs.

In Iowa, where the race was delayed by wrangling over the caucus date, there were fears the money would not flow. But once the timeline was set, WHO, the NBC affiliate, along with another Des Moines station, took in nearly $3.5 million in the last weeks of 2011. A local station manager admitted he was prepared to interrupt his New Year's Eve dinner to upload new political ads. In all, more than $12.5 million worth of advertising was purchased in the Iowa race, and December 2011 revenues for WHO were up more than 50 percent from December 2010. The driver in the frenzy of last-minute TV advertising in Iowa and New Hampshire was the Super PACs.

Warping the Process

Super PAC advertising is not like traditional campaign advertising. As the scenario that played out in Iowa illustrates, Super PACs allow allies of candidates with the right connections to the right CEOs and hedge-fund managers to pile up money that can then be used not to promote that candidate but to launch scorched-earth attacks on other candidates. The scenario is particularly well suited to negative advertising. This warps the process in a perverse way, creating a circumstance where a candidate who is not particularly appealing to voters but who *is* particularly appealing to a small group of 1 percenters can, with the help of well-funded friends, frame a campaign in his favor.

The threat to democracy plays out on a number of levels. Candidates without the right connections may prevail in traditional tests—as Gingrich did with strong debate performances and Rick Santorum did with grassroots organizing and a solid finish in Iowa. But they are eventually targeted and taken out by the Super PACs, and the candidate with the right connections, in this case Romney, enjoys smooth sailing. In Iowa, roughly 45 percent of all ads aired on local TV stations: thousands of commercials, one after another, attacking Gingrich.

Negative advertising can be effective even if it does not generate a single new voter for the candidate favored by the Super PAC placing the ad. If negative ads simply scare off potential backers of an opponent, that's a victory. Moreover, negative ads often force targeted candidates to respond to charges, no matter how spurious. And our lazy and underresourced news media allow the ads to set the agenda for coverage, thereby magnifying their importance and effect.

The most comprehensive research to date concludes that between 2000 and 2008 the overall percentage of political TV ads that were negative increased from 50 percent to 60 percent. And 2008 is already beginning to look like a tea party. The percentage and number of attack ads in 2010 were "unprecedented," and they are increasing sharply again in 2012.

"I just hate it, and there's so much of it," Sarah Hoffman complained to a reporter at a Gingrich event in the Iowa town of Shenandoah. "Anytime they do anything negative, I just turn it off." Gingrich emerged as a born-again reformer for about ninety-six hours during his Iowa free-fall, telling voters like Hoffman: "It will be interesting to see whether, in fact, the people of Iowa decide that they don't like the people who run negative ads, because you could send a tremendous signal to the country that the era of nasty and negative thirty-second campaigns is over."

To the extent that campaigns are covered, the focus is on personalities and the catfight character of the competition.

The Effect on Voters

If a signal was sent from Iowa, it was that many voters would rather switch off than try to sort out the attacks. With no competition on the Democratic side, and with conservatives supposedly all ginned up to choose a challenger for President Obama, Republicans confidently suggested that caucus turn-out would rise from 119,000 in 2008 to as much as 150,000 in 2012. Instead, turnout was up only marginally, to around 122,000. If the maverick candidacy of Ron Paul had not attracted thousands of new voters to the caucuses—many of them antiwar and pro-civil liberties independents unlikely to vote Republican in the fall—the turnout would almost certainly have fallen to pre-2008 levels. "If all people hear are negatives, a lot of them are just going to ask, Why bother?" says Ed Fallon, a former Democratic legislator and local radio host in Des Moines who caucused this year as a Republican. "And they're even more frustrated by the fact that the money for the negative campaigning comes from all these unidentified sources on Wall Street."

The research of scholars Stephen Ansolabehere and Shanto Iyengar demonstrates that the main consequence of negative ads is that they demobilize citizens and turn them away from electoral politics. This fact is a "tacit assumption among political consultants," they explain, arguing that the trend is toward "a political implosion of apathy and withdrawal."

The Role of the News Media

Were national and local broadcast media outlets to cover politics as anything more than a horse race and a clash of personalities, they might be able to undo much of the damage. But stations across the country—and the newspapers they often depend on for serious coverage—have eviscerated local reporting in recent years. Surveys suggest that news programs now devote far less time to political coverage than they did twenty or thirty years ago. To the extent that campaigns are covered, the focus is on personalities and the catfight character of the competition. So it was that when Gingrich complained about the battering he was taking from the Super PACs, the story was portrayed as a dust-up between a pair of candidates rather than as evidence of a structural crisis. In part, this is the fault of the candidates, who for the most part do not want to speak too broadly about Super PAC abuses in which they are engaging or in which they hope to engage.

Once it became clear that the media had no real interest in examining the problem, Gingrich quickly got with the program. Rather than make an issue out of campaign corruption, Gingrich's own Super PAC, Winning Our Future, corralled a $5 million donation from the spare-change drawer of Las Vegas casino mogul Sheldon Adelson (listed by *Forbes* as the eighth-wealthiest American, with a $21 billion fortune) just before the New Hampshire primary. The plan was to launch a blitzkrieg against Romney. Here we finally get the proper metaphor for post-*Citizens United* elections: mutually assured destruction, with citizens and the governing process the only certain casualties.

Unwitting Allies

Unfortunately, the media outlets that could challenge this doomsday scenario tend to facilitate it. The elimination of campaign coverage is masked to a certain extent because the gutting of newsrooms also encourages what sociologist Herbert Gans describes as the conversion of political news into campaign coverage. As campaigns have become permanent, so has campaign coverage. Such coverage is cheap and easy to do, and lends itself to gossip and endless chatter, even as it sometimes provides the illusion that serious affairs of state are under scrutiny. To someone watching cable news channels, it might seem that presidential races have never been so thoroughly exhumed by reporters. But the coverage is as nutrition-free as a fast-food hamburger. After a panel of "experts" finish "making sense" of Rick Perry's debate performances, political ads don't look so bad.

> *The real clash is between money and democracy. And the media outlets that continue to play a critical role in defining our discourse are not objecting. They are cashing in.*

With the little news coverage that remains focusing overwhelmingly on the presidential race, Congressional, statewide and local races get little attention nationally or even locally. Not surprisingly, research suggests that political TV advertising is even more effective further down the food chain. "In presidential campaigns, voters may be influenced by news coverage, debates or objective economic or international events," the Brookings Institution's Darrell West explained in 2010. "These other forces restrain the power of advertisements and empower a variety of alternative forces. In Congressional contests, some of these constraining factors are absent, making advertisements potentially more important. If candidates have the money to advertise in a Congressional contest, it can be a very powerful force for electoral success."

West's point is confirmed by a simple statistic from the 2010 races: of fifty-three competitive House districts where Rove and his compatriots backed Republicans with "independent" expenditures that easily exceeded similar expenditures made on behalf of Democrats—often by more than $1 million per district, according to Public Citizen—Republicans won fifty-one.

To the extent that media outlets cover campaigns, they highlight the "charge and countercharge" character of the fight as an asinine personality clash between candidates. But the real clash is between money and democracy. And the media outlets that continue to play a critical role in defining our discourse are not objecting. They are cashing in. Meanwhile, citizens are checking out.

9

Why *Citizens United* Has Nothing to Do with What Ails American Politics

Ilya Shapiro

Ilya Shapiro is a senior fellow in constitutional studies at the Cato Institute.

There are a number of major misunderstandings about the Supreme Court Citizens United *decision.* Citizens United *will not open the floodgates for special interests or foreign corporations to spend unlimited money to influence American elections. It also didn't affect laws regarding individual or corporate contributions to political candidates. It will, however, give smaller groups more influence. If there are reforms to be made to the current system, it should be to completely eliminate limits on individual contributions and then require disclosures for big donors. This will improve both transparency and accountability.*

*C*itizens United is one of the most misunderstood Supreme Court decisions ever. It doesn't stand for what many people say it does.

Take, for example, President Obama's famous statement that the decision "reversed a century of law that I believe will open the floodgates for special interests—including foreign corporations—to spend without limit in our elections." In one sentence, the former law professor made four errors of law.

First, *Citizens United* didn't reverse a century of law. The president was referring to the Tillman Act of 1907, which prohibited corporate donations to candidates and parties. *Citizens United* didn't touch that. Instead, the overturned precedent was a 1990 case that, for the first and only time, allowed a restriction on political speech based on something other than the appearance of corruption.

Second, the floodgates point depends on how you define those terms. As even the July 22 *New York Times* magazine reported, there's no significant change in corporate spending this cycle. There are certainly people running Super PACs who would otherwise be supporting candidates directly, but *Citizens United* didn't cause Super PACs (as I'll explain shortly). And the rules affecting the wealthy individuals who *are* spending more haven't changed at all. It's unclear that any "floodgates" have opened or which special interests didn't exist before.

Third, the rights of foreigners—corporate or otherwise—is another issue about which *Citizens United* said nothing. Indeed, just this year the Supreme Court summarily upheld the restrictions on foreign spending in political campaigns.

Fourth and finally, while independent spending on elections now has few limits, candidates and parties aren't so lucky, and neither are their donors. Again, *Citizens United* didn't affect laws regarding individual or corporate contributions to candidates.

More important than *Citizens United* was *SpeechNow.org v. FEC*, decided two months later in the D.C. Circuit. That ruling removed limits on donations to political action committees, thus making these PACs "super" and freeing people to pool money the same way one rich person can alone.

And so, if you're concerned about the money spent on elections—though Americans spend more on chewing gum and Easter candy—the problem isn't with big corporate players. That is another misapprehension: Exxon, Halliburton, and all these "evil" companies (or even good ones) are not suddenly dominating the political conversation. They spend little money on political advertising, partly because it's more effective to lobby, but mostly because they wouldn't want to alienate half of their customers. As Michael Jordan famously said, "Republicans buy shoes, too."

Political money is like water: it'll flow somewhere because what government does matters and people want to speak about their concerns.

On the other hand, groups composed of individuals and smaller players now get to speak: Your National Federations of Independent Business and Sierra Clubs, your ACLUs and Planned Parenthoods. So even if we accept "leveling the playing field" as a proper basis for regulation, the freeing of associational speech levels that field. Moreover, people don't lose rights when they get together, be it in unions, advocacy groups, clubs, for-profit companies, or any other way.

Nevertheless, various bills and constitutional amendments have been proposed to remedy some of *Citizens United*'s perceived ills. The idea behind these efforts is that elections will be cleaner if we can only eliminate private campaign money.

The underlying problem, however, isn't the underregulation of independent spending but the attempt to manage political speech in the first place. Political money is like water: It'll flow *somewhere* because what government does matters and people want to speak about their concerns. To the extent that "money in politics" is a problem, the solution is to reduce the political scope that the money can influence. Shrink government, and you'll shrink the amount people spend trying to get a piece of the pie.

While we await that shrinkage, we do have to address the core flaw in the campaign finance regime. That original sin was committed by the Supreme Court not in *Citizens United* but in the 1976 case of *Buckley v. Valeo*. By rewriting the Watergate-era Federal Election Campaign Act to remove spending limits but not contribution caps, *Buckley* upset Congress's balanced reform.

That's why politicians spend all their time fundraising. Moreover, the regulations have pushed money away from candidates and toward advocacy groups—undermining the worthy goal of government accountability.

The solution is obvious: Liberalize rather than restrict the system. Get rid of limits on individual contributions and then require disclosures for those who donate amounts big enough for the interest in preventing corruption to outweigh the potential for harassment. Then the big boys will have to put their reputations on the line, but not the average person. Let voters weigh what a donation's source means to them, rather than allowing politicians to write rules benefiting themselves.

We now have a system that's unbalanced and unworkable. At some point, however, there will be enough incumbents who feel that they're losing message control to such an extent that they'll allow fairer political markets. Earlier this summer, for example, the Democratic governor of Illinois signed a law allowing unlimited contributions in races with significant independent spending. This deregulation is an act of political self-preservation, but that's fine.

Once more politicians realize that they can't prevent communities from organizing, they'll want to capture more of their dollars. Stephen Colbert would then have to focus on other laws to lampoon, but I'm confident that he can do that and we'll be better off on all counts.

Ultimately, the way to "take back our democracy"—to invoke the name of the campaign-finance hearing at which I recently testified—isn't to further restrict political speech but to rethink the basic premise of existing regulations.

10

Super PACs Spur Negative Political Advertising and Distort American Politics

Richard L. Hasen

Richard L. Hasen is a blogger, professor at University of California Irvine College of Law, and the author of The Voting Wars: From Florida 2000 to the Next Election Meltdown.

Super PACs have emerged as a real danger to the American political landscape. These organizations can accept unlimited contributions from individuals, corporations, and labor unions to spend in favor of specific candidates. Much of that spending comes in the form of negative ads, which saturated the airwaves before the 2012 presidential election. The proliferation of Super PAC spending is particularly troubling in Senate and congressional races, where large amounts of money can sway candidates away from the public interest and distort American politics.

This election season, the term "Super PAC" [political action committee] has escaped from the obscure world of campaign finance lawyers to emerge on the front pages of major newspapers and political websites. Super PACs are political organizations that can take unlimited sums from individuals, corporations and labor unions to spend in support of, or opposition to, federal candidates. To do so legally, a Super PAC must avoid certain forms of coordination with candidates.

The groups played a big role in Iowa, with a pro-Mitt Romney Super PAC, "Restore Our Future," widely credited with running ads that halted Newt Gingrich's momentum in the polls. They are expected to play an even greater role in the fall, when control of the White House, Senate and U.S. House of Representatives will be up for grabs.

The Dangers of Super PACs

Super PACs are troublesome for a number of reasons.

They tend to run more negative advertising, since they are able to act as the "evil twin" of campaigns because they are not accountable to voters the way candidate committees are. Thanks to holes in our disclosure laws, which neither Congress nor the Republican commissioners on the Federal Election Commission have seen fit to fix, we don't know who is funding many of the Super PACs.

Candidates can even raise money under certain conditions for supportive Super PACs without violating the FEC's technical coordination rules. And thanks to clever campaign finance lawyers who can use an affiliated nonprofit 501(c)(4) group, we may never know the identity of some donors. (That's why comedian Stephen Colbert formed his 501(c)(4) "Colbert Super PAC SHH" (as in "hush") to funnel money to his regular "Colbert Super PAC")

But the greatest danger of Super PACs is that they may skew the legislative process in the next Congress in favor of the interests of large Super PAC contributors.

Citizens United

To understand why, we need to go back to the Supreme Court's controversial 2010 opinion in *Citizens United v. Federal Election Commission*. In that case, the Supreme Court held that the First Amendment barred a federal law preventing corporations and unions from spending their own funds to influence the outcome of elections. Key to this ruling was the court's statement that independent spending (that is, spending not coordinated with candidates) cannot corrupt the political process.

From there, lower courts and the FEC, spurred by opponents of campaign finance regulation, led the way for the creation of Super PACs. As I have explained, first they concluded that if independent spending cannot corrupt, then an individual's contributions to an independent group cannot corrupt. (Gone was the $5,000 per person contribution limit to political action committees—or PACs—which only spend independently to support or oppose federal candidates.)

Federal officeholders may do the bidding of other wealthy individuals, corporations and labor unions out of fear that they will support the official's opponents through a Super PAC in the next election if they don't.

Second, they concluded that if an individual's contributions to one of these Super PACs cannot corrupt, then neither can a corporation's or a labor union's contribution. (Corporations now have a way to influence elections anonymously, thus avoiding the risk of alienating customers who may object to their choice of candidates.)

But the initial supposition is wrong. Independent spending can corrupt.

Selling Influence

The main reason the Supreme Court has rejected challenges to campaign contribution limits (currently set at $2,500 per election to federal candidates) is that large contributions can create the actuality and appearance of corruption of those candidates. A candidate who receives a large contribution will feel grateful to the contributor, and legislative policy could well skew in the contributor's direction.

Well what of the six- and seven-figure donors to Super PACs supporting federal candidates? Federal officeholders are likely to feel just as indebted to them. And federal officeholders may do the bidding of other wealthy individuals, corporations and labor unions out of fear that they will support the official's opponents through a Super PAC in the next election if they don't.

Given the expected vast spending by presidential candidates and parties in the general election, I am not very concerned that Super PAC spending will influence the outcome of the presidential election, though it might.

I am not even that concerned about Super PAC negative advertising, which can serve to educate the public and mobilize some voters to become more politically engaged.

But I am concerned that Super PAC spending will influence the outcome of close Senate and congressional races. And I am greatly concerned that when Election Day is over and the public will stop hearing about Super PACs, contributions to these groups will skew public policy away from the public interest and toward the interest of the new fat cats of campaign finance, as members of the House and Senate thank their friends and look over their shoulder at potential new enemies.

11

Super PACs Benefit Politics and Do Not Lead to Nastier Campaigns

Jonathan Alter

Jonathan Alter is an author and political columnist and commentator.

There has been widespread concern that Super PACs would seriously damage the US political system by having individual donors contribute large amounts of money to support certain candidates, buy unlimited influence with the campaign, and saturate the airwaves with dirty attack ads. In the 2012 presidential campaign, however, donors who contributed money to Super PACs that went on to air nasty attack ads experienced blowback from the media, customers, and colleagues. These donors found out that large donations to Super PACs had consequences, often damaging business relationships and alienating their customer base.

Strangely enough, the 2012 presidential campaign, expected to be the dirtiest in modern memory, may end up being relatively clean.

That's because both sides agree that the economy is the central issue and that sideshows like the Reverend Jeremiah Wright aren't persuasive for voters. Karl Rove and Larry McCarthy, the creator of the infamous Willie Horton ad, think harsh personal attacks against President Barack Obama will backfire, and they're offering more subtle messages of economic disappointment instead.

Even economic assaults can boomerang nowadays. Newark Mayor Cory Booker, an otherwise strong Obama supporter, dealt the Obama campaign a blow last weekend on NBC's "Meet the Press" when he said he was "nauseated" by an Obama ad lambasting Mitt Romney's tenure at Bain Capital LLC. The president's defense of the ad, in which he said "there are folks who do good work" in private equity, was too complicated to be effective.

The controversy surrounding the Bain ad and a proposed Wright ad from a super-PAC [political action committee] backed by Joe Ricketts, the billionaire founder of TD Ameritrade Holding Corp. (AMTD), suggests that when "paid media" in the presidential race ventures out-of-bounds, "free media" will exact a penalty. (House and Senate races are another story.)

When it's not clear who the attacker is, the old rule in politics that attack ads hurt the attacker as well as the target is rendered obsolete.

Avoiding the Gutter

We can still expect a misleading and overwhelmingly negative campaign, but the distortions and outright lies will be mostly about the candidates' records and positions, not their race, religion and standing as patriotic Americans. I don't mean to be pollyannaish, but that represents a step up from the gutter.

The days when Lyndon Johnson could use the infamous "daisy ad" to suggest Barry Goldwater wanted to blow up the world, or Vice President George H.W. Bush (and Al Gore before him) could exploit the racist Willie Horton story against Michael Dukakis, are over. In 2004, when Swift Boat Veterans for Truth could easily smear John Kerry's character by distorting his Navy service during the Vietnam War, you couldn't yet use YouTube and blogs to rebut an ad and even organize a boycott of the sponsors within hours. If the Swift Boat attacks aired today, President George W. Bush would probably be forced to denounce them.

This sounds counterintuitive. After the Supreme Court's *Citizens United* decision, the campaign system is awash in super-PACs and shadowy 501(c)(4)s (dubbed "spooky-PACs" by Stephen Colbert) that allow secret donations. Instead of clearly identifying the origin of the ad ("I'm Mitt Romney, and I approve this message"), the tag lines on the super-PAC ads are from gauzy-sounding outfits ("Restore Our Future") that few people recognize. When it's not clear who the attacker is, the old rule in politics that attack ads hurt the attacker as well as the target is rendered obsolete.

As we learned during the Republican presidential primaries, this has changed the tone of the campaign. About 70 percent of the ads in the presidential campaign from January 1, 2011, to April 22, 2012, contained at least some negative content, according to the Wesleyan Media Project, which, not coincidentally, found that more than half of Romney's ads were funded by super-PACs. Obama will have plenty of money for his own negative ads, but he will be responsible for most of them ("I'm Barack Obama, and I approve this message"). Romney, meanwhile, can at least theoretically avoid accountability.

Keeping Clean

But neither candidate can afford to let his backers wander too far off the reservation. When Ricketts considered running a super-PAC ad featuring Obama's relationship with his former pastor Wright, known for his controversial views, the proposed commercial (aimed at stripping the president of his stature as a "metrosexual, black Abe Lincoln") leaked to the

New York Times. The fallout may cost the Ricketts family trust, which owns the Chicago Cubs, as much as $150 million, which is real money even for a billionaire. That's the amount the team was seeking from the City of Chicago to help fund the renovation of Wrigley Field. A furious Mayor Rahm Emanuel wouldn't even return phone calls from the Ricketts family, and the Wrigley Field deal is probably dead.

Aside from the hypocrisy of free-market conservatives seeking taxpayer money for their sports businesses (routine across the country), the Ricketts story sends a powerful message to other billionaires trying to play in the presidential election sandbox: Expect sand in your eyes.

The best way to avoid it—and stay on good terms with the Romney campaign (which sees anything racial or personal about the president as counterproductive)—is to go with approved (though technically not "coordinated") super-PACs and spooky-PACs like those run by Rove and a group of Romney's former top aides. That's what Texas plutocrats like Harold Simmons and Robert Perry, original Swift Boaters, are doing this year.

Rove's American Crossroads and Crossroads GPS, which so far this election cycle have raised more than $100 million, will probably have at least a couple hundred million to use trashing Obama—often unfairly. But most of it will be spent on depicting the president as incompetent on the economy, not on personal attacks.

So the Ricketts episode, while harmful to Romney in the short run, helps him down the road by giving billionaires incentive to stay on the same page as the campaign.

The near-universal condemnation of the proposed Wright ad also increases the likelihood that any comments about Romney's Mormon faith will be seen as off-limits.

I've long argued that when you're talking about the most powerful job in the world, all biographical facts—relationships with old pastors, management of companies, religious practices, even old girlfriends—are at least potentially relevant. But this year, with the country facing a stark choice in hard times, they will be derided as distractions from an unusually substantive campaign.

Organizations to Contact

The editors have compiled the following list of organizations concerned with the issues debated in this book. The descriptions are derived from materials provided by the organizations. All have publications or information available for interested readers. The list was compiled on the date of publication of the present volume; names, addresses, phone and fax numbers, and e-mail and Internet addresses may change. Be aware that many organizations take several weeks or longer to respond to inquiries, so allow as much time as possible.

Accuracy in Media (AIM)
4455 Connecticut Ave. NW, Suite 330, Washington, DC 20008
(202) 364-4401 • fax: (202) 364-4098
e-mail: info@aim.org
website: www.aim.org

Accuracy in Media (AIM) is a nonprofit, grassroots citizens' watchdog of the news media "that critiques botched and bungled news stories and sets the record straight on important issues that have received slanted coverage." The organization finds examples of liberal media bias in print, television, and other media; provides an analysis of biased stories, political speeches, and campaign ads and counters misinformation and distortions; and coordinates media conferences, lectures, and symposiums to discuss the subject of media bias and develop strategies to facilitate a more balanced US media. The AIM website features blogs, audio and video of speakers and experts, commentary, and special reports.

Center for Competitive Politics (CCP)
124 West St. S, Suite 201, Alexandria, VA   22314
(703) 894-6800 • fax: (703) 894-6811
website: www.campaignfreedom.org

The Center for Competitive Politics (CCP) is an organization that fights national, state, and local regulations against political speech. CCP defends political speech, including negative campaign ads, through research projects, educational efforts, strategic litigation, lobbying at national and state levels, and activism. The group provides legal representation for parties looking to strike down campaign laws that restrict free speech through the court system. The CCP website features a range of information on the group's recent efforts, including research, speeches and testimony from CCP employees, a blog, and commentary on relevant topics and strategies.

Center for Media and Democracy (CMD)

520 University Ave., Suite 260, Madison, WI   53703
(608) 260-9713 • fax: (608) 260-9714
website: www.prwatch.org

The Center for Media and Democracy (CMD) is a nonprofit investigative group that exposes the ways in which the media is influenced by corporate spin and government propaganda. One of its recent investigations focused on the American Legislative Exchange Council (ALEC), a conservative group created to draft and advocate for business-friendly policies and legislation. The CMD website features in-depth reports on corporate media influence, campaign finance, negative campaigns ads, the banking scandal, election fraud, and other pertinent subjects. It also offers updates on recent initiatives, breaking news, regular and guest commentary, a video archive, and access to *SPIN*, the Center's e-newsletter.

Center for Media and Public Affairs (CMPA)

933 N. Kenmore St., Suite 405, Arlington, VA   22201
(571) 319-0029 • fax: (571) 319-0034
e-mail: mail@cmpa.com
website: www.cmpa.com

An affiliate of George Mason University, the Center for Media and Public Affairs (CMPA) is an independent research and educational organization that provides "an empirical basis for ongoing debates over media coverage and impact through well-documented, timely, and readable studies." The CMPA emphasizes a scientific approach to media research, differentiating it from other media watchdog groups. One of CMPA's main efforts has focused on improving the election process. Recent studies, which are available on the CMPA website, include the use of political humor in media coverage and science and health reporting.

Center for Political Accountability (CPA)

1233 20th St. NW, Suite 205, Washington, DC   20036
(202) 464-1570 • fax: (202) 464-1575
e-mail: mail@politicalaccountability.net
website: www.politicalaccountability.net

The Center for Political Accountability (CPA) is a nonprofit, nonpartisan group formed to bring accountability and transparency to corporate political contributions by encouraging companies to disclose details of their political spending. In the wake of the *Citizens United* ruling, CPA also has focused on the danger of Super PAC spending and its influence on American politics. The CPA website offers updates on the group's efforts, including breaking news, commentary and op-eds written by CPA fellows, and recent press releases. It also features current and archived issues of the CPA newsletter, reports and surveys, legal briefs, and comprehensive background information on the rules legislating corporate political spending.

The Center for Public Integrity

910 17th St. NW, Suite 700, Washington, DC   20006
(202) 466-1300
e-mail: communications@publicintegrity.org
website: www.publicintegrity.org

Founded in 1989, the Center for Public Integrity is one of the largest nonpartisan news organizations in the United States. Its mission is to expose abuses of power, corruption, and lies perpetrated by powerful individuals and corporations. One of its main interests is the role of money in US political campaigns and its influence on the American political system. In recent years, the Center for Public Integrity has investigated the impact of Super PACs on national, state, and local elections and has pursued greater transparency and accountability for such groups. Information on the Center's investigations can be found on the organization's website, which also features opinion and commentary and access to the Center's weekly e-newsletter.

Common Cause

1133 19th St. NW, 9th Floor, Washington, DC   20036
(202) 833-1200
e-mail: CauseNet@commoncause.org
website: www.commoncause.org

Common Cause is a nonprofit advocacy group dedicated to enhancing accountability in the political process and encouraging citizen participation in American democracy. Common Cause is a citizens' lobby that works to bring about long-term reforms; an educational organization that engages the public and the press on the need for greater transparency and accountability; and a grassroots activist group. One of its major initiatives is the push to pass legislation to undo the *Citizens United* decision. The Common Cause website offers updates on recent efforts and access to reports, filings, testimony, letters, commentary, and research.

FactCheck.org

Annenberg Public Policy Center, 202 S. 36th St.
Philadelphia, PA   19104
(215) 898-9400
e-mail: Editor@FactCheck.org
website: www.factcheck.org

FactCheck.org is a project of the Annenberg Public Policy Center established to provide independent fact-checking services for American voters. The nonprofit group focuses on reducing the level of misinformation and confusion in US political campaigns—especially in political advertising, speeches, interviews, and statements. FactCheck.org is regarded as one of the premier fact-checking organizations in the country. The project's website features analysis of current controversies and Internet rumors, archives of past investigations, and answers to readers' questions.

Media Matters for America

445 Massachusetts Ave., Suite 600, Washington, DC   20001
(202) 756-4100
website: www.mediamatters.org

Media Matters for America is a web-based nonprofit research organization that works to monitor and correct conservative misinformation and propaganda in print, television, radio, or the Internet media. They accomplish this through opinion pieces, research, and in-depth studies of conservative programming and campaign ads and speeches. On the Media Matters website, they feature a blog to address breaking issues, video clips of instances of conservative misinformation, and their own programming to analyze pertinent stories. They also publish a number of newsletters and media alerts that offer readers the latest news and updates on relevant stories.

PolitiFact

490 First Ave. South, St. Petersburg, FL   33701
(727) 893-8111
website: www.politifact.com

A project of the *Tampa Bay Times*, PolitiFact has become a highly regarded fact-checking organization that analyzes statements by members of Congress, the White House, lobbyists, and interest groups. The reporters and editors that work at PolitiFact assess the accuracy of this information, rating it on the Truth-O-Meter for its level of veracity. During the 2012 presidential election, PolitiFact was very active in analyzing statements made on the campaign trail and during debates. The PolitiFact website offers access to weekly e-mails that include updates and articles on recent analyses.

Bibliography

Books

L. Brent Bozell and Tim Graham
Collusion: How the Media Stole the 2012 Election—and How to Stop Them from Doing It in 2016. New York: HarperCollins, 2013.

Greg Elmer, Ganaele Langlois, and Fenwick McKelvey
The Permanent Campaign: New Media, New Politics. New York: Peter Lang, 2012.

Dennis W. Johnson
Campaigning in the Twenty-First Century: A Whole New Ballgame? New York: Routledge, 2011.

Jason Johnson
Political Consultants and Campaigns: One Day to Sell. Boulder, CO: Westview Press, 2012.

Lawrence Lessig
Republic, Lost: How Money Corrupts Congress—and a Plan to Stop It. New York: Twelve, 2011.

Keena Lipsitz
Competitive Elections and the American Voter. Philadelphia: University of Pennsylvania Press, 2011.

Thomas E. Mann and Norman J. Ornstein
It's Even Worse than It Looks: How the American Constitutional System Collided with the Politics of Extremism. New York: Basic Books, 2012.

John Nichols and Robert W. McChesney — *Dollarocracy: How the Money-and-Media Election Complex Is Destroying America*. New York: Nation Books, 2013.

Lynn Hudson Parsons — *The Birth of Modern Politics: Andrew Jackson, John Quincy Adams, and the Election of 1828*. New York: Oxford University Press, 2009.

Larry J. Sabato, ed. — *Barack Obama and the New America: The 2012 Election and the Changing Face of Politics*. Lanham, MD: Rowman & Littlefield, 2013.

Daniel M. Shea — *Can We Talk? The Rise of Rude, Nasty, Stubborn Politics*. New York: Pearson, 2013.

Jeffrey Toobin — *The Oath: The Obama White House and the Supreme Court*. New York: Doubleday, 2012.

Periodicals and Internet Sources

John Avlon and Michael Keller — "The Super-PAC Economy," *Daily Beast*, September 18, 2012. www.thedailybeast.com.

John Steele Gordon — "Gingrich and the History of Negative Campaigns," *Wall Street Journal*, January 4, 2012.

Bob Greene — "Mudslinging Campaigns Hurt the Economy," CNN.com, September 2, 2012. www.cnn.com.

Joe Hagen — "The Coming Tsunami of Slime," *New York*, January 22, 2012.

Jared Keller — "When Campaigns Manipulate Social Media," *Atlantic*, November 10, 2010.

Andy Kroll — "In the Future, Everyone Will Have a Super-PAC," *Mother Jones*, January 28, 2013.

Ruthann Lariscy — "Why Negative Political Ads Work," CNN.com, January 2, 2012.

Norman J. Ornstein — "Effect of *Citizens United* Felt Two Years Later," *Roll Call*, January 18, 2012.

Rosemarie Ostler — "A Look Back: In Spite of Super PACs, This Isn't the Most Negative Campaign in History," *Christian Science Monitor*, February 2, 2012.

Steven Rosenfeld — "How Super PACs Warped the 2012 Election," *AlterNet*, November 9, 2012. www.alternet.org.

Jack Shafer — "Looking for Truth in All the Wrong Places," Reuters, August 31, 2012. www.reuters.com.

Bradley A. Smith — "Why Super PACs Are Good for Democracy," *U.S. News & World Report*, November 17, 2012.

James Warren — "Fact-Checking Campaign Lies: Does Anybody Give a Damn?," *Atlantic*, September 4, 2012.

Peter Wehner — "Some Historical Perspective on Negative Campaigning," *Commentary*, October 29, 2010.

William E. White   "The Will of the People," *Huffington Post*, August 14, 2012. www .huffingtonpost.com.

Index